ARMORED IN SUBMISSION

Wives Unlocking Victory in Marriage Through Surrender

TAMMINN S. TRAIL

T.S.TRAIL

Manhasset, New York

Published by T.S. Trail
Manhasset, New York

ISBN: 979-8-9931021-0-8

Cover design by T.S. Trail
Printed in the United States of America

This book is written to inspire and encourage through biblical truths and personal testimony. It is not intended as a substitute for professional counseling or legal advice.

To my beloved Zoe, whose name means *life*.
For thirty-three weeks, your heartbeat pulsed within me,
giving me life as I carried yours. You never took a breath on
earth, but your presence awakened something eternal in me.
This book is your legacy—written from the place where grief
and glory met. Through you, God rekindled a holy fire within
me that continues to burn for Him day after day.

"In him was life, and that life was the light of all mankind."
— John 1:4 (NIV)

CONTENTS

Preface VI

Acknowledgements VIII

Introduction ix

1. Kingdom and Covenant 1

2. The Wars and the Bride... 10

3. The Vision, Mission and Mandate 22

4. Know the Real Enemy 33

5. The War Room: Strategic Prayer Planning.................. 43

6. Chain of Command: Honoring God's Order 68

7. The Armor of a Warrior Bride... 77

8. Tactical Communication 89

9. Field Intelligence: Knowing Your Spouse 103

10. The Art of Adaptability..117

11. Leading from the Rear: Strenght of Support............124

12. Morale Maintenance: Keeping Joy in the Journey..132

13. Logistics of Love: Managing the Home Front........145

14. Allies and Advisors: Seeking Godly Counsel 153

15. The Will to Withstand: Cultivating Resilient Faith 160

16. Post-War Reconciliation & Healing................................169

17. Raising Warriors: Marriage as Ministry 177

18. Conclusion 205

19. About the Author 208

PREFACE

This book was born out of one of the most painful seasons of my life. At thirty-three weeks pregnant, Heaven gained my daughter, Zoe. Her heart stopped beating before she ever took her first breath. The grief was indescribable. What made it even more incomprehensible was knowing that my husband and I had asked God for this child with such intentionality. We prayed not simply for another baby of our own, but for a child who would fulfill God's divine purpose on earth. We were specific in our request: "Lord, do not allow us to conceive unless this life will serve Your Kingdom."

When Zoe's heart stopped, I was broken. In those days of grief, I wrestled with questions and pain. But in that same place of brokenness, the Lord spoke to me. He told me He was going to do something greater with me. He said,

> "I'm going to do you one better. You will still multiply life. You will multiply yourself by multiplying what Zoe represented. Not only will you raise your own children, but through your life, and your obedience, you will raise children across the world to love Me, to fear Me, and to walk in My ways. As you multiply yourself as a wife, as a mother, and as My daughter, you will transform homes and rescue families across the world."

That word shifted me. It awakened a fire in me that has been blazing ever since. My Father used my most excruciating pain to birth me into purpose.

Soon after, He confirmed it in a tangible way. My sister in the faith reached out and asked me to speak at her upcoming Wives Conference called *Wives Wage War*. This was the first assignment I accepted since saying goodbye to Zoe. But I knew it was no coincidence. It was God's confirmation of what He had spoken.

As I prepared to minister to those wives, the Lord began to pour out revelation after revelation. I realized He wasn't just giving me a message for one event. He was giving me a battle plan. Page by page, prayer by prayer, this book took form as the fruit of both my pain and my surrender.

Armored in Submission: Wives Unlocking Victory in Marriage Through Surrender is that fruit. It carries the lessons God gave me in the valley, the principles He showed me about marriage and warfare, and the calling He placed on my life to multiply myself so that His Kingdom would be advanced through marriage and families around the world.

This book is more than words on paper. It is my obedience to what the Lord asked of me, and it is an offering for every wife who is ready to discover that submission is not bondage, but armor. That victory in marriage is not distant, but already secured in Christ.

ACKNOWLEDGEMENTS

This book is the fruit of a lifetime of love, prayers, and voices that have spoken into me long before I ever sat down to write. Those I mention here may not even know the role they played, but their presence, encouragement, and example have shaped me in ways that overflow onto these pages. With a grateful heart, I offer these acknowledgements.

To my incredible husband, Tyrone. Thank you for loving me in every season. Your strength, humility, and quiet leadership are gifts I treasure. You are my safe place.

To my precious children, Nala, Micah, and to Zoe in Heaven. This is for you. You give me joy and fuel my calling.

To my beautiful mother, Joan. You love me unconditionally and continually speak life into me. I don't know what I would do without you. To my beloved sisters and brothers, and to all my friends and family, your love anchors me. Daily you remind me of who I truly am.

I give honor to my spiritual father, Bishop Victor J. Lewis, Sr., now in Heaven, who saw the assignment of marriage and family on my life and affirmed my calling before he transitioned to glory. The seeds you planted continue to bear fruit in my life every day.

To my cherished church family, the Friendship Baptist Church of Roslyn, Inc. Thank you for covering me. Your love and fellowship are dear to my heart. I am grateful for you.

To every person who has ever prayed for me, cheered me on, or simply loved me faithfully, please know that your impact lives here too.

And to every woman walking this journey with me, thank you. You are seen, called, and empowered. Let us continue to unlock victory in marriage and family together.

INTRODUCTION

Marriage was never designed to be a battlefield between husband and wife. It was designed to be a covenant where two people join forces under God's authority. But more than that, marriage was designed to reveal a mystery: the union between Christ and His Church. When we lose sight of this, we reduce marriage to personalities and preferences, and we miss the greater vision God tied to it.

This truth changed my own marriage. When my husband and I realized that our covenant was not just about us, but about Christ and His Bride, it shifted our mindsets. Our love, our forgiveness, our endurance, and even our submission took on new meaning. My marriage to my husband is meant to reflect Christ's love for His Church and the Church's response to Him. That understanding has helped me fight differently, not against my husband, but for the mission God has entrusted to us. Our union carries a vision, mission, and mandate. And when we see it that way, we fight from a place of purpose, not pain.

This book was formed through that journey; learning that victory doesn't come from striving harder, but from surrendering deeper. Not surrender to dysfunction or defeat. But surrender to the One who authored covenant and gave us the blueprint for how to walk it out.

When a wife submits herself to the Lord, she comes under His covering, His wisdom, and His strategy. From that position, submission within her marriage is not weakness, as culture may suggest. It is her place of strength, safety, and authority. Submission becomes her armor; her God-given posture for preserving unity, advancing love, and securing victory in her home.

This is not a book of band-aid solutions. It is not a list of techniques to change your husband or tips to simply survive until he understands you. This is a call to step into your purpose as a wife who is both a builder and a warrior, anchored in Christ and clothed in honor. This is about unlocking victory by putting on the armor of submission and fighting differently: with prayer, faith, not against your husband, but for him.

In the chapters ahead, we will explore military principles and kingdom truths that will reframe how you see both marriage and spiritual warfare. As you lean into these lessons, you won't just learn strategies; you will begin to see the fruit of surrender come alive in your home:

- Your marriage will be secured like a fortified post, not easily shaken by outside attacks, because you are covered by God.

- You will walk with clarity and discernment, no longer blindsided by the enemy's schemes, but equipped to guard your home with peace and confidence.

- Your prayers will carry undeniable authority and power, shifting the atmosphere of your home and drawing God's presence closer.

- Honor will flourish in your covenant, creating a safe refuge where love, respect, and trust multiply.

- You and your husband will rise in true oneness, moving together in purpose and reflecting Christ and His Church.

- And your joy will be undeniable. Not the fragile happiness the world chases, but the deep, sustaining joy of the Lord that makes your marriage a place of laughter, friendship, and delight.

As you walk in these truths, your perspective will shift. You will not see yourself as a weary wife, but as a woman of valor, anchored in Christ, and clothed in the armor of submission. Submission will not diminish you; it will anchor you. The joy of the Lord will fill your covenant, as you and your husband move together in the greater vision, mission, and mandate God has entrusted to your union. Victory in your marriage is not something you strive to win; it is the reality you already possess in Christ. And as you yield to Him, you will realize that you have already won.

ONE

KINGDOM AND COVENANT

The Foundation — Understanding the Kingdom

Whenever we fight, it is because something valuable is on the line. A soldier fights to protect his country. A mother fights to protect her children. In marriage, the fight should be no different. As a wife, when you fight, it must be with the mindset that you are protecting your husband, your covenant, and what God has entrusted to you. This is not simply about preserving happiness or fixing problems. It is about ensuring that the Kingdom of God remains established in your home. When Jesus came, He came with peace and power. He came to save, comfort, but also to establish order. The Kingdom of God is not just a place; it is Heaven's rule in action. It is God's structure, His leadership, and His divine order breaking into the earth. And it must be made real in every part of your life, your marriage, your parenting, your purpose, and your legacy.

The Kingdom of God is where God's will become the way things are. It's not just spiritual talk; it's spiritual structure. It's the authority of Heaven being carried out on earth through people who God chose. It's not just about what happens after you transition from earth. It's about how you live right now; submitted to God's leadership. Jesus preached, "Repent, for the Kingdom of Heaven is at hand." (Matthew 4:17, ESV). He wasn't just telling people to stop sinning. He was saying: "Turn around. You've been

1

following the world's way, but now Heaven's way is here. You can live under a new system."

To truly walk in the Kingdom, we must know Jesus not only as Savior, but also as Lord. Salvation introduces us to His grace, but His Lordship calls us into surrender. Many believers stop at salvation, rejoicing in being rescued from sin, yet resisting His authority over their daily lives. But a life in the Kingdom is not simply about being saved from something, it is about being governed by Someone. Jesus said:

> "Abide in me, and I in you. As the branch cannot bear fruit by itself, unless it abides in the vine, neither can you, unless you abide in me. I am the vine; you are the branches. Whoever abides in me and I in him, he it is that bears much fruit, for apart from me you can do nothing" (John 15:4–5, ESV).

Abiding is the picture of submission. When we refuse to let Jesus reign as Lord, we reject that abiding connection. And without submission, there can be no true surrender. Lordship means His word shapes our choices, His Spirit leads our steps, and His will defines our lives. This is the posture of the Kingdom, Jesus enthroned not just in Heaven, but in us.

When you submit your marriage to God, you're not just asking Him to fix things. You're bringing your home under His government. You're inviting His order into your everyday life, and that's where true transformation happens.

The Kingdom is Built on Covenant

Just as an earthly kingdom has laws and a constitution, God's Kingdom has a foundation as well. But His foundation isn't built on rules first, it's built on relationship. God doesn't force us to obey so He can love us. He loves us first, then invites us into covenant. That's how His Kingdom works. A covenant is a sacred promise. It's God saying, "I'm committed to you, and I'll never break My Word." And when we say yes to Him, we become part of His system. We receive His covering, His protection, and His instructions. When God builds something, whether it's a nation, a church, or a marriage' He starts with a covenant.

Isaiah 9:6 says, "For to us a child is born, to us a son is given; and the government shall be upon his shoulder..." (ESV). This verse is about Jesus. And it tells us something powerful: The Kingdom is not confined to a throne in Heaven; its government rests on Christ's shoulders. He bears the responsibility, because real love comes with real responsibility. Marriage also bears responsibility. It's not just a partnership or a romance. It's a covenant structure where the Kingdom is supposed to manifest. When God sees your marriage, He doesn't just see two people in love, He sees a place where Heaven can rule. That's why your position matters. When you walk in alignment with God, your home becomes a spiritual embassy. Your prayers are effective. Your words shape the atmosphere. Your obedience opens doors; not just for you but for your entire household.

In our home, this truth has its own expression. My husband and I are originally from Jamaica, and though our children were born here in the U.S., Discipline and order are pretty different from what we are used to; we often jokingly tell them: "The moment you step through these doors, you're no longer on American soil, you've entered the Jamaican embassy." It gets a laugh, but they know what we mean. The discipline, the order, the expectations; they're different here because our house is run by a different government.

Sometimes, our kids will ask, "How come other kids get to do that, and we can't?" And we tell them gently: "They don't live here, and we're not their parents." Not because those parents are wrong but because God has given different families different instructions. What works for one house may not work for another. Our job is to follow what God has assigned to us. That's how the Kingdom works, too. When your house belongs to God, it doesn't operate like the culture outside. Your marriage, your parenting, your decisions—they're not supposed to blend in. They're supposed to reflect Heaven. You don't have to be perfect to walk in that kind of authority. You just need to be in position and surrendered to Jesus as your Lord.

Covenant Families — God's Chosen Structure

If the Kingdom of God is His government on earth, then covenant is the way He chooses to establish and sustain it. A covenant is not a contract. It's not just an agreement or a handshake. It is sacred. It is spiritual. And it is sealed with sacrifice. In Scripture, covenants weren't just made; they were cut. They involved blood, they marked territory, and they weren't just personal; they were generational. Every time God wanted to build something that would last, He started with a covenant. He didn't begin with rules, or with armies. He began with relationship that came with responsibility. That's what makes covenant different than casual commitments. When God resets or advances something in Scripture, look closely, it always involves families in covenant.

Noah: Covenant After the Storm

Let's look at Noah. After the flood, God didn't just save Noah. He saved Noah's household, his wife, his sons, and their wives (Genesis 9). The ark wasn't a solo rescue; it was a family vessel. Even the animals entered in pairs. Fruitfulness required alignment. Multiplication required structure. God didn't send Noah back out alone. He made a covenant with him and sealed it

4

with a sign: the rainbow. But look again, God didn't just speak to Noah. He said: "I now establish my covenant with you and with your descendants after you." (Genesis 9:9, NIV). Covenant was always meant to flow through marriage and family.

Abraham: Covenant of a Nation

Now, look at Abraham and his covenant. When God called Abraham, He didn't promise him just a private blessing. He promised a nation, a people, a lineage, and a spiritual bloodline. "In you, all the families of the earth shall be blessed." (Genesis 12:3, ESV). But Abraham had questions. "How will I know?" he asked. And God responded with something profound—a blood covenant. God told Abraham to bring specific animals and cut them in half, placing the halves opposite each other. This was not a random ritual. In ancient Middle Eastern culture, this act was how covenants were sealed between two parties. The two people entering the agreement would walk between the pieces together. It was a way of saying, "May this be done to me if I break my word." The split animals symbolized the consequence of breaking the covenant.

But here's what's astounding: Abraham didn't walk through the pieces. God caused a deep sleep to fall upon him (Genesis 15:12). And instead of Abraham walking through, two symbols appeared: a smoking firepot and a flaming torch, representing the presence of God. They passed between the pieces alone, which reveals something profound: God made the covenant with Himself. Why? Because He knew man could never perfectly uphold his side of the agreement. Abraham's responsibility was to believe. If this covenant was going to last, it had to be carried by God alone. So, He made the promise and bore the full weight of keeping it. He was saying, "If this covenant fails, let the penalty fall on Me."

This is one of my favorite covenants in all of scripture because of its depth, its beauty, and what it foreshadows. It was a prophetic glimpse of the cross. Jesus Christ would later fulfill this covenant by becoming the sacrifice. He took on our failure and bore the consequences in His own body. He became both the promise-maker and the promise-keeper. That's the kind of covenant we're in. Not one based on our performance but on God's unshakable love and faithfulness.

Jesus: Covenant Fulfilled and Forever

Jesus didn't just preach about the Kingdom. He sealed it in His blood. Every covenant before Him pointed forward to what He would do. He didn't cancel them. He completed them. When He lifted the cup at the Last Supper, He said: "This cup that is poured out for you is the new covenant in my blood." (Luke 22:20, ESV) This was more than symbolic. It was legal. Eternal. Final.

Through Jesus, we didn't just get access to Heaven; we were brought into God's royal family. Now, every wife, every husband, and every child who enters covenant with Christ becomes part of His divine plan to establish Kingdom order on earth. You're not just in a relationship with God. You're in covenant. And if your marriage is also a covenant, then your household has governmental responsibility in the spirit, with fruit that manifests in the earth.

The Pattern of Legacy

Every time God made a covenant, He had more in mind than just the moment. Covenant was never about the individual alone; it was about the generations that would come through them. God's heart has always been for legacy, and godly legacy flows through families that are aligned with His Kingdom. This is why your marriage matters so much. It is not just the beginning of a love story; it is the beginning or the continuation of a spiritual lineage.

When you and your husband enter covenant with each other and with God, you become conduits through which Kingdom legacy can flow. God's pattern has never changed: He starts with a person. He builds a family. And through that family, He establishes His presence in the earth.

Moses: A Covenant That Formed a Nation

Through Moses, God didn't just set individuals free from slavery. He formed an entire nation. A people set apart. He gave them laws, structure, and identity. He gave them a tabernacle to host His presence and a priesthood to represent His holiness. But take a closer look, God didn't give His instructions to priests alone. He spoke to fathers, mothers, and children. The commandments were to be taught in homes, discussed at the dinner tables and passed down from generation to generation. "Impress them on your children. Talk about them when you sit at home and when you walk along the road..." (Deuteronomy 6:7, NIV). The Kingdom was never meant to stay in the temple. It was meant to also live in the house. And that's still true today. Your home isn't just a residence; it's a Kingdom training ground. Your living room is where legacy takes root.

David: A Covenant of Authority

God made a covenant with David that one of his descendants would sit on the throne forever. "I will raise up your offspring after you... and I will establish the throne of his kingdom forever." (2 Samuel 7:12-13, ESV). That promise pointed straight to Jesus. But it also revealed something powerful: Covenant produces kings. It produces heirs. It produces authority. When you say yes to covenant, you're not just saying yes to intimacy. You're saying yes to inheritance.

In Christ, you've been made royalty, seated with Him in heavenly places (Ephesians 2:6). Your home has spiritual jurisdiction. You are not just cohabiting; you are co-ruling. Your prayers, your decisions, and your obedience all matter in the Kingdom and carry eternal consequences. This is why Satan fights covenant marriages so fiercely. When a couple walks in agreement with God, they become dangerous to the kingdom of darkness. They raise up seeds and pass down wisdom that outlives them.

Forgiveness — The Doorway to Covenant

When we think of covenant, we often think of promises, purpose, and power. But at the core of every covenant God made—with Noah, with Abraham, with Israel, and now with us, was something more tender: forgiveness. We don't enter covenant because we deserve it. We enter because He made a way. And that way is Jesus. It was sealed with blood. The blood that produced forgiveness. The blood that continually cleanses us, restores us, and keeps us inside the covering of covenant. That's why the words in Lamentations 3:22–23 are so moving: "The steadfast love of the Lord never ceases; his mercies never come to an end; they are new every morning; great is your faithfulness." (ESV).

Mercy is the posture of a covenant carrier. You can't walk in covenant without walking in forgiveness, both receiving it and extending it. That's how God governs His Kingdom. And that's how we must govern our homes. Whether you're navigating marriage, motherhood, or just life, covenantal living requires mercy at every turn. Because without mercy, we forfeit the flow of grace. Without mercy, we forget the foundation we're standing on.
You are standing on mercy. And if God has built your life and your covenant on mercy, then it means this, you're never disqualified from beginning again.

So, what do you do with this revelation of Kingdom and Covenant? You align, you receive, you forgive. You govern your home accordingly.

It was essential for me to explain all of that before we arrived at this point. I hope you followed. The Bible says, "In all your getting, get understanding." Proverbs 4:7 (KJV). I wanted to provide this foundational information in the first chapter because knowing it helps us tighten our armor, allowing us to fight from our position of victory.

In the next chapter, we will examine the War in Heaven, the first recorded war in the Bible on earth, and see how it connects to the Bride of Christ and you as a bride. But first, let's pray and do some self-reflection on this chapter.

Prayer
Father, thank You for the blood that speaks a better word. Thank You for Your mercy that didn't give up on me. Today, I receive that mercy again, and I ask for help to give it freely. Let my life reflect the covenant I've been invited into. Jesus, be Lord over my home. Govern us, lead us, and establish Your Kingdom within our walls. In Jesus' name, Amen.

Journal Reflection
Where have I struggled to believe that mercy still covers me?

Who have I refused to extend covenant-level forgiveness to?

What part of my marriage or home needs to be brought under God's Kingdom rule again?

TWO

THE WARS AND THE BRIDE

Before you ever fought a battle in your home, a war was already fought in Heaven. Before the arguments, the tears, and the confusion, long before marriage even existed on Earth, the enemy had already declared war on everything that reflected the image of God. That includes marriage. That includes family. That includes you. The battles you're facing in your marriage are not random. They are not simply the result of personality clashes, unmet expectations, or poor communication. They are echoes of an ancient conflict. A war much older than your wedding day.

The First War in Heaven: A Broken System

Scripture pulls back the veil and reveals a cosmic reality, "Now war arose in heaven, Michael and his angels fighting against the dragon. And the dragon and his angels fought back, but he was defeated..." (Revelation 12:7–8, ESV) Satan, once radiant and glorious, lifted himself in pride and rebelled against God's order. As a result, he was cast down to Earth, and Scripture declares: "Woe to you, O earth and sea, for the devil has come down to you in great wrath because he knows that his time is short!" (Revelation 12:12, ESV). The rebellion in Heaven fractured creations perfect alignment with God's order. And Satan, filled with fury, has been waging war against what God loves most ever since: unity, covenant, legacy.

The Garden Invasion: How Satan Targeted Marriage

Satan's rebellion touched humanity in Eden. Satan was not content to fall alone. Because he cannot create, he corrupts. Because he fell from purpose, he seeks to cause others to fall from theirs. And so, after his rebellion in Heaven, he set his sights on the very ones made in God's image. In Genesis 3, we see him in the Garden, speaking not to Adam but to Eve. He sowed doubt, distrust, and disobedience, not just against God but within marriage itself. Adam, who was called to lead and protect, instead followed Eve's decision, and the order of marriage was disrupted. What Satan could not destroy in Heaven, he tried to destroy on Earth, beginning with the very first marriage covenant. I want you to grasp this fact right here:

- Satan's rebellion fractured creations perfect alignment with God's order. `

- He now wages war against covenant structures, especially marriage, because they reflect Heaven's government.

Satan does not need to invent new tactics. He simply repeats the same cycle: seduction, deception, rebellion, and fall. What he experienced; he seeks to recreate. He fell from alignment; therefore, he attacks yours. He fell from purpose, so he tempts you to abandon yours.

There is something startling in Genesis 3 when God addressed the woman after the fall:

> "To the woman he said, 'I will surely multiply your pain in childbearing; in pain you shall bring forth children. Your desire shall be contrary to your husband, but he shall rule over you." (Genesis 3:16, ESV).

There is such a deep revelation here. The curse reduced women to only physical childbearing. Even though pain was multiplied, we could still produce children. That part of fruitfulness remained. But the greater purpose, the spiritual assignment, the divine mission that is tied to husband and wife walking together in agreement, was fractured. God had given mankind the command:

> "And God blessed them. And God said to them, 'Be fruitful and multiply and fill the earth and subdue it, and have dominion over the fish of the sea and over the birds of the heavens and over every living thing that moves on the earth.'" (Genesis 1:28, ESV)

Fruitfulness was never meant to stop at the womb. It was also about mission, purpose, and dominion. But the curse divided desire. The woman's desire would pull against her husband's, and he would rule over her. Two different desires, two different directions. And the Word is clear: "Can two walk together, except they be agreed?" (Amos 3:3, KJV). Without spiritual agreement, fruitfulness is limited to having children, and a greater mission is lost. This is why many couples can have children yet struggle to produce beyond that, because agreement was broken at the fall. Without one desire, purpose and mission dissolve into conflict.

Satan gave to man what he carried himself. His desire was contrary to the purpose God created him for. He and God could no longer walk together because they no longer agreed. When Adam and Eve ate of the tree at Satan's word, he transferred that divided desire to them, and division became their inheritance.

Jesus: Heaven's Restoration Plan

But here is the hope. Jesus restored what was lost. At the cross, the curse was broken, and mission was given back. Now we can pray:

12

"Lord, give me Your desires, and give them also to my husband. Align our hearts so that we walk together in oneness."

When we receive God's desires, we receive more than a marriage, we receive a mission and a mandate (we'll talk more about this in the next chapter). Agreement is restored and fruitfulness multiplies again.

God was not caught off guard. Even before Satan's fall, even before Adam and Eve stumbled, the Lamb was already slain in the plan of God.

"The Lamb who was slain before the foundation of the world." (Revelation 13:8, ESV).

Jesus came to restore what was broken:

- The curse was shattered.

- The blueprint was reinstated.

- The government of Heaven was reestablished on earth.

In Christ, unity is our restored inheritance. Now as husband and wife, we do not only multiply children. We multiply spiritually. We multiply in purpose. We multiply in legacy. Through Christ, you are no longer surviving marriage; you are called to steward it as a holy, strategic assignment under God's divine order.

The First War on Earth: A Rescue Mission

Genesis 14 records the first physical war ever mentioned in Scripture: Four kings waged war against five. Kingdoms clashed. Territories were seized. Amid the chaos, Lot and his entire household were taken captive. This is where revelation meets reality. The enemy wasn't just after land. He wasn't just after possessions. He took family. It has always been the enemy's pattern to disrupt, divide, and steal households. The true spoils of spiritual warfare have always been the next generation; but Abram (later Abraham) didn't stay complacent. He rose up.

- He assembled 318 trained men.

- He pursued the enemy with strategy and courage.

- He fought not for personal gain but to recover his family.

He refused to accept the loss. He refused to allow the enemy to write the final story. And when victory came, Abram refused to take the spoils of war. He made it clear that this battle wasn't about power. It was about covenant. It wasn't about riches; it was about restoring what God ordained.

Wives, hear this, the enemy's goal has never changed. Just like in Abraham's day, he is after your family. He comes to raid the marriage covenant, seize spiritual inheritance, and fracture future generations. But God is still raising up sons and daughters like Abram, those who will pursue, overtake, and recover all. And you are one of them.

David at Ziklag: Another Pattern of Rescue

The same strategy and the same rescue appear again in the life of David. In 1 Samuel 30, David and his men returned to their city, Ziklag, only to find that while they were away, the Amalekites had raided it. Their wives, sons, and daughters had all been captured. Everything precious was stolen. Their homes were burned. Their hearts were crushed. David could have been paralyzed by grief. He could have surrendered to despair. But he didn't. David did something prophetic: "And David inquired of the Lord, 'Shall I pursue after this band? Shall I overtake them?' He answered him, 'Pursue, for you shall surely overtake and shall surely rescue.'" (1 Samuel 30:8, ESV). David sought the counsel of God, and God's response was immediate: Pursue. Overtake. Recover all. David obeyed. He pursued the raiders. He fought. And he recovered everything that had been stolen—wives, children, future legacy intact.

Spiritual Insight: God's Faithfulness to Rescue

Across generations, the pattern is clear:

- The enemy targets families.

- God raises up rescuers.

- Restoration is not just possible, it is promised, secured, and made available to you in Christ.

In your marriage, in your home, in your motherhood; you are standing in the same spiritual storyline. You shall overcome all the attacks, and you are rising with Heaven's commission to pursue, overtake, and recover all.

Temporary Roles, Eternal Purpose

One day, I realized something that changed how I fight for my marriage and raise my children. In eternity, my husband will no longer be my husband, and my children will no longer be my children. In heaven, there is only one Bridegroom, and we are all His bride. There is only one Father, and we are all His children. That realization made me ask: What am I really fighting to protect in my marriage? What is family truly about?

The answer was clear: marriage has never been about me. It has always been about God. My role as a wife is not about my comfort, my fulfillment, or even my husband's response. It's about reflecting Christ and His relationship with His Church. My role as a mother is not about my pride in raising children, it's about stewarding the Father's heart. These roles are temporary assignments, entrusted to me as tools for something eternal.

When the Sadducees asked Jesus about a woman who had been married to multiple brothers, His response revealed this truth: "For in the resurrection they neither marry nor are given in marriage but are like angels in heaven" (Matthew 22:30, ESV). Marriage as we know it does not exist in heaven. Parenthood as we know it does not exist in heaven. But while they are temporary on earth, they carry eternal purpose. They are meant to honor God, to reflect His Kingdom, and to reveal His order in the earth.

This truth reframes everything. If I reduce marriage to personal fulfillment and happiness instead of reflecting Christ and His Church, I distort the very picture it was created to reveal. If I parent for my own pride rather than the Father's glory, I misrepresent His heart. And if I live as though these roles exist for me rather than for God, then I have missed their purpose entirely.

This is why certain battles are not worth fighting. When you understand that your fight is not about winning arguments but about aligning with God, your strategies shift. Your fight is set up differently. And when you live this way, joy and peace are not things you chase; they flow naturally because you are walking in step with God's design.

If you are single and you desire marriage, pause and consider why you desire it. Is it just for you, or is it for God? Because if it is not for Him, it does not matter how happy you feel, you will still fail. Your definition of winning could still be failure in the sight of God. Scripture tells us "…whatever you do, work at it with all your heart, as working for the Lord, not for human masters" (Colossians 3:23, NIV). This is not to scare you out of marriage; it is to empower and equip you. The right thing done for the wrong reasons is still rejected by God. I believe you would rather be rejected by man and the world but be eternally accepted by God.

Marriage and the Ekklesia: A Picture of the Bride

It's no coincidence that after every rescue and every restoration, God calls His people back to identity and government. Marriage reflects divine government. It is an embassy of Heaven planted on earth. When Jesus spoke to Peter about building on the rock, He didn't say, "I will build My temple" or "I will build My synagogue." He declared: "I will build My *Ekklesia*" (Matthew 16:18, ESV). The word *Ekklesia* in Roman and Greek culture referred to a governing assembly, citizens called out to legislate, make decisions, and carry the authority of the kingdom they represented. When Jesus said, "I will build My *Ekklesia*," He was establishing His government on earth through a called-out Bride. Not a building with stained glass and pews, but an assembly armed with His authority, His Word, and His Spirit to carry out the will of Heaven. The Church is both:

- A called-out Bride, beautiful and beloved
- A governing force, strategic and authoritative

Marriage mirrors this divine structure. As wives, this means we are not secondary participants in marriage. We are strategic agents of Kingdom culture. Our submission is placement; coming under Heaven's authority, where our strength becomes unstoppable.
When you understand this, mirroring the Church's role in your marriage becomes easier. Just as the Church is called to yield to Christ in trust and reverence, so the wife is called to submit to and honor her husband. Marriage becomes a living picture of the Bride's response to the Bridegroom.

17

"Wives, submit yourselves unto your own husbands, as unto the Lord. For the husband is the head of the wife, even as Christ is the head of the church: and he is the saviour of the body. Therefore, as the church is subject unto Christ, so let the wives be to their own husbands in every thing" (Ephesians 5:22–24, KJV).

When you embrace this, your perspective shifts. Submission feels like alignment. Honor no longer feels like an obligation; it feels like worship through obedience and devotion. Marriage no longer feels like a struggle to be understood; it becomes a sacred classroom where God is training you to reflect the posture of His Bride.

Repentance: Realigning with Heaven's Blueprint

When we grasp the depth of what was broken and the greatness of what Christ restored, there is only one rightful response: Humble, wholehearted repentance. A surrender that says:

"Father, I repent for receiving a broken image of marriage from a broken world. I repent for resisting Your divine order. I repent for calling disorder freedom. Open my eyes to Your Kingdom blueprint. Show me how to build, stand, and fight according to Your divine design. I choose Your order over my opinion. I choose Your government over my emotions. Let my marriage be a living embassy of Your Kingdom on Earth."

Because unless we see this clearly, we will continue losing battles we were already destined to win.

God's Blueprint for Marriage: A Divine Commission

Marriage is not man's invention; it is Heaven's design.

God's blueprint is not a suggestion; it is a divine constitution for victory. Below, you will find things that are a part of God's blueprint.

1. *Covenant, Not Contract* – Marriage is a sacred, binding vow sealed before God, not a flexible agreement based on feelings (Malachi 2:14; Ephesians 5:31–32).

2. *Two Become One* – Marriage is about merging lives, destinies, and spiritual callings into one divine assignment (Genesis 2:24).

3. *Christ and the Church* – Marriage mirrors the sacrificial love of Christ and the trusting honor of the Church (Ephesians 5:22–33).

4. *Order and Roles Rooted in Love* – Leadership and submission function not through dominance but through covenantal love (Ephesians 5:21; 1 Peter 3:7).

5. *Fruitfulness* – Marriage is designed to produce both natural and spiritual fruit, multiplying God's legacy across generations (Genesis 1:28).

6. *Forgiveness and Grace* – Covenant is sustained through the flow of constant forgiveness and mercy (Colossians 3:13; Ephesians 4:32).

7. *Centered on Christ, Not Each Other* – The marriage is strong not because husband and wife are perfect but because both are tethered to Christ (Matthew 22:37–40).

8. *Shared Mission and Vision* – Marriage is a partnership in advancing Heaven's agenda, not just enjoying earthly comforts (Amos 3:3; Matthew 28:19–20; Genesis 1:28).

When you align your marriage with God's blueprint, you are not just repairing a relationship; you are rebuilding a stronghold for Heaven's purposes.

A Posture of Hunger

In this season, God is calling His daughters to hunger for righteousness above all. Victory doesn't come by accident. It comes by desire.

- Desire for God's way over your own way.

- Desire for divine alignment over emotional convenience.

- Desire for righteousness over resentment.

When righteousness becomes your craving, recovery becomes your reality. You are called to be a wife who hungers for the right things, not to be right, but to be righteous. And in doing so, you will not only rescue your home, but you will also rebuild it into a testimony of God's glory.

To rebuild, you must first know what you're building toward. Every rescue has a mission, and every wife must understand the vision and mandate behind her fight. We'll unpack that in the next chapter.

Prayer:

Father, stir a fresh hunger in me for Your ways. Teach me to thirst for righteousness more than validation. Awaken a craving in me to see my marriage through Your eyes, not the world's lens. I submit my heart and my desires to Your divine order. Help me to remain in Your will and satisfy me with the joy of living in alignment with You. In Jesus' name, Amen.

Journal Reflection

Where in my heart or home have, I unknowingly accepted a broken version of marriage?

What would it look like for me to truly crave God's blueprint above my own ideas?

THREE

THE VISION, MISSION AND MANDATE

What Are You Really Fighting For?

Every battle begins with a vision. Without one, soldiers march without direction, expend energy without purpose, and suffer losses without gain. Marriage is no different. Many wives find themselves weary. Not because they've stopped fighting but because they've forgotten why they started. Before we can talk about armor or communication tactics, we must ask a foundational question: what am I really fighting for in my marriage?

- Peace in my home?
- Emotional closeness with my husband?
- A godly legacy for my children?
- The healing of past wounds?
- Something bigger than just me and my spouse?
- All the above?

How will you know when the war is over and if you've even won? The clarity of your vision will determine the strength of your pursuit. In war, soldiers don't fight for the sake of conflict; they fight because something precious is at stake: freedom, family, and the future. The same is true in marriage. When a wife understands what she's protecting, her pain begins to serve a purpose. A godly marriage involves two people being holy and united in love and honor. Your union has the potential to transform generations. When Satan attacks marriage, he's not just coming after your togetherness; he's targeting your legacy. Look at it this way: When you have a clear vision of what your marriage is supposed to look like, every challenge becomes part of a larger story God is writing through you.

A Personal Revelation: Marriage as Assignment

For my husband and me, this became deeply personal. We examined our family histories and noticed a troubling pattern: marriage wasn't common. On both sides, we noticed divorce, separation, or simply a lack of lasting unions. We realized we weren't just building a marriage; we were breaking cycles. We were fighting against generational patterns that said marriage doesn't last. That awareness gave us strength. It made us realize that God didn't just bring us together to be happy; He brought us together to start a legacy.

If I'm being completely honest, marriage wasn't something I deeply longed for. Though I wasn't against it either. It wasn't popular in the world I grew up in, and it wasn't modeled for me in a way that made me hunger for covenant. I can only recall two couples whose marriages I admired, one being a friend and the other my brother. For the most part, I was okay with being loved and respected, even if that meant living with someone unmarried for the rest of my life. At that time, I wasn't saved. I didn't understand the assignment. I didn't understand the sacredness of the covenant.

But then God intervened. Marriage was given to me purely by His grace; unearned, unexpected, and undeniably divine. This helped us to realize we'd been called to serve Him in this area, and we began to see the purpose of our marriage with greater clarity:

- To restore honor to the covenant of marriage as a reflection of Christ and His Church

- To model godly love and leadership that shapes our children and empower those we influence

- To multiply faithfulness, fruitfulness, and spiritual order across generations

- To build families and communities that reflect Heaven's culture on earth

Our children will grow up desiring not just any relationship, but a marriage rooted in God. And that's worth fighting for.

When You Can't See the Destination

For many of us, we're praying hard, showing up every day, and doing our best, yet we still feel worn out, confused, or directionless. Not because we don't love our spouse but because we've lost sight of the destination. Or maybe we never had one. In war, a soldier without a clear vision becomes exhausted. And in marriage, a wife without vision becomes vulnerable to discouragement. "Where there is no vision, the people perish..." (Proverbs 29:18, KJV).

Vision is more than a plan or a dream. It's a prophetic glimpse of what God desires your marriage to become. It is God's destination, revealed from Heaven, not imagined in your emotions. Just as Moses was shown the Promised Land, a place flowing with milk and honey. You also must see where your marriage is supposed to go. Not where you want it to go. Not where culture says it should go. But where God ordained it to go. You must ask: "Lord, what do You see when You look at our marriage?" Until you receive God's vision, you may find yourself fighting battles that don't matter and missing victories that do.

Blueprint: Vision, Mission, and Mandate

God doesn't call us to fight blindly. Every marriage that has kingdom authority must have Heaven's design:

- *Vision* – The destination. What does God want this marriage to become?

"Where there is no vision, the people perish." (Proverbs 29:18, KJV)

- *Mission* – The reason. Why did God bring us together?

"For we are his workmanship, created in Christ Jesus for good works, which God prepared beforehand, that we should walk in them." (Ephesians 2:10, ESV)

- *Mandate* – The spiritual authority to carry it out. What have we been assigned to build and protect?

"And God blessed them. And God said to them, 'Be fruitful and multiply and fill the earth and subdue it, and have dominion...'" (Genesis 1:28, ESV)

These three are not just concepts. They are the war strategy of your marriage. Without them, even love can feel lost. But with them, your pain begins to serve purpose, your efforts align with eternity, and your steps are led by revelation.

The Key to Clarity

I realized something remarkable that has changed my life. The more I desired God's order for my marriage and pursued it, the more satisfied I became as a wife. The more peace and joy fill my home. I absolutely love the Beatitudes. You may notice them appear often throughout this book. They are weapons I lean on, especially when the war is within myself in the process of becoming. One says, "Blessed are those who hunger and thirst for righteousness, for they shall be satisfied" (Matthew 5:6, ESV).

The kind of satisfaction God promises isn't about everything feeling easy. It's about everything becoming aligned. When you hunger, not for perfection but for righteousness, you're crying out to be realigned with Heaven's vision, Heaven's order, and Heaven's strategy. You're saying, "God, I don't want a marriage that just works. I want a marriage that reflects You." And when that becomes your hunger, He will satisfy it. He will reveal the blueprint. He will give you strength to pursue it. And He will pour grace to build it.

Abraham: Lifting His Eyes to Legacy (Vision)

When God gives you a *vision*, it's never just about the present; it's about the future. When He called Abraham, it wasn't just to bless a man; it was to birth a nation. The scriptures tell us there came a moment when the land could no longer sustain both Abraham and his nephew Lot. Their households began to argue and collide. So, Abraham chose separation. But what came after that moment of surrender was something sacred. "The Lord said to Abram after Lot had separated from him, 'Lift up your eyes… for all the land that you see I will give to you and to your offspring forever.'" (Genesis 13:14–15, ESV)

In that moment, Abraham wasn't just seeing land. He saw legacy. He was seeing nations, promises, and a spiritual lineage that would stretch beyond time. He was seeing you. He was seeing me. He was seeing generations of covenant keepers and purpose walkers. That's what vision does. Vision lifts your eyes beyond barrenness. When Abraham looked into the night sky, he saw no son in his tent but stars in the heavens. And still, God said, "Count them, if you can... So shall your offspring be." (Genesis 15:5, ESV) He didn't have Isaac yet. But he had vision. And vision gave him the strength to endure waiting, obedience, and sacrifice.

Jacob: Fighting for Legacy and Position (Mission)

Then there's Jacob, Abraham's grandson, whose story reminds us that vision often requires a fight. Jacob loved Rachel. He worked for her for seven years but was deceived and given Leah instead. (Genesis 29) Many would have stopped there. Many would've settled, assuming disappointment meant denial. But Jacob labored another seven years for the one his heart truly loved. Through Rachel came Joseph. Through Leah came Judah. And here's where the *mission* reveals itself in full, Joseph would one day save Israel during a famine. Judah would become the bloodline of Jesus, the Lion of the Tribe of Judah. But if Joseph had not preserved the Tribes of Israel... there would be no Judah. And if not through Judah, then through whom would Jesus have come?

The tribe was chosen, because the story of redemption was never random. Jacob wasn't just fighting for romance; he was in purpose, fighting for redemption. He didn't even know it, but everything was strategic. That's what the mission looks like. Mission doesn't always feel glamorous. It often looks like working through deception, fighting for clarity, and laboring for what's been promised. But when God gives you a mission, it is never in vain.

Joseph: Guarding the Mandate of Redemption

Joseph's life was marked by betrayal, abandonment, and injustice. Yet he remained faithful. Why? Because he carried a *mandate*: to preserve a people, to protect a promise, and to position the bloodline of Christ. Mandate isn't about ambition. It's about assignment. It's what God has authorized you to carry and protect, no matter what you walk through. Joseph wasn't promoted to second-in-command in Egypt for status. He was positioned there to preserve his brothers, especially Judah, whose descendants would include Jesus. And here's the mystery of God: in Genesis 37:26–27, it was Judah who first preserved Joseph's life, urging his brothers not to kill him but to sell him instead. Long before Joseph saved Judah, Judah saved Joseph. Even then, God was orchestrating legacy and preparing a safe passage for Christ.

The mandate resting on their lives meant neither of them would die prematurely because the lineage of the Messiah was being carried forward through both obedience and divine orchestration.

Your marriage is not just about your happily ever after. It's about preservation. You are protecting what God intends to birth, not just through you but through those who come after you. Like Joseph, you've been sent ahead to prepare the ground. You've been positioned in marriage to safeguard something holy.

Jesus: The Fulfillment of Every Family Battle

Every fight for vision, every mission endured, every mandate protected, it was all pointing to one Person: Jesus.

- Jesus was the reason Abraham needed vision.
- Jesus was the reason Jacob had to pursue his mission.
- Jesus was the reason Joseph had to protect the mandate.

28

Because the ultimate marriage, the union between Christ and His Bride, was always the end goal. And now, God is using your marriage to echo that same story. You are not just part of a covenant. You are participating in the fulfillment of Heaven's family plan.

What This Means for You

This is why you can't quit. This is why your posture matters. This is why you must protect peace, fight for clarity, and contend in the spirit. Because this isn't just about today; it's about generations to come. Your legacy, your obedience, your resilience. All of it is part of Heaven's redemptive story. You're not just a wife; you are a silent force in legacy warfare. Your marriage is meant to:

- Model God's faithfulness by reflecting His steadfast love in the way you build, forgive, and endure

- Multiply legacy and identity by raising a family that knows who they are in Christ and carries His name with honor

- Host God's presence by cultivating peace, prayer, and purity in your home

- Advance Kingdom influence on the earth by letting your marriage become a living testimony of unity, strength, and divine order

That satisfaction that God wants to give you in your marriage won't come from ease. It will come from alignment. When your desire is to be in divine order, God will fill you. He will lead you. And He will use you.

What if You're Fighting Alone?

There may come a moment in marriage where you realize you're the only one contending. The only one praying. The only one trying. The only one asking for help. And the weight of that reality can make you feel like the battle is already lost. But I want to tell you something I learned in my own walk: God often builds the woman while the man is unaware. He did it in Eden. Adam was asleep when God formed Eve. He crafted her carefully, intentionally, from his side. Adam didn't participate. He didn't even know it was happening. And yet, when he awoke, he saw her fully formed. Finished. Whole.

He did it again on the cross. After Jesus finished His work on the cross, He gave up His Spirit and rested in death; a soldier pierced His side. From that wound flowed blood and water. Redemption and cleansing. It was almost as if His water broke. A flow that symbolized something new being birthed: the beginning of a cleansed people, His Bride, His Church rising from sacrifice. And here's the truth: Sometimes, your obedience is the warfare. You don't have to drag your husband into the fight to win the battle. God sees your position. He honors your posture. And He works while others sleep.

This is not about staying in a harmful or abusive situation. This is about spiritual endurance in seasons where the mission is still active, but the other party isn't showing up. And if that's you, I want to remind you that you are not alone, you are not forgotten, and you are not fighting in vain. God builds in silence, He forms in stillness, and He is doing something in you that your husband may not see yet, but when he does, it will not be the same woman he left behind. He will behold the radiance of who you've become. Like Eve, formed while no one was watching. Like the Church, flowing from the side of Christ. Like you—rising in quiet surrender.

So, if you're fighting alone, remember this: Faithfulness is a weapon, obedience is armor, and transformation is often born in secret. Stay in position until God says otherwise. You are not losing. You are being formed.

Every assignment attracts opposition. And to carry your mandate well, you must discern who you're really fighting. In the next chapter, we'll uncover the true enemy of your marriage and the strategy behind his attacks.

Prayer

Father, I come before You with a new hunger, not just for answers, but for alignment. Open my eyes to see what You see in my marriage. Give me clarity of vision, strength for the mission, and grace to carry the mandate. Let me hunger and thirst for righteousness in my role as a wife. Let my posture, my words, and my heart reflect Heaven's design. Where I have grown weary, restore me. I surrender again to Your call, and I receive the blueprint for this covenant. In Jesus' name, Amen.

Journal Reflection

Intentionally seek God, and ask Him to reveal the vision, mission and mandate of your marriage.

Vision:
Where is your marriage going?
What does the 'Promised Land' of your marriage look like when seen through God's eyes?

Mission:
Why did God bring you together?
What are you uniquely called to build, restore, or demonstrate as a couple?

Mandate:
What are you charged to protect and multiply?
What spiritual or generational inheritance is your marriage carrying for others?

FOUR

KNOW THE REAL ENEMY

Misplaced Battles in The Fog of War

There is a term in military combat known as *"the fog of war."* It describes the confusion, miscommunication, and uncertainty that can cloud a soldier's judgment in the middle of a battle. Visibility is low. The noise is high. And in that disoriented state, soldiers have been known to shoot their own teammates, mistake signals, or retreat when they should stand. The enemy loves the fog. Because when vision is blurred, and targets are unclear, he doesn't need to overpower you; he just needs to let you turn on each other.

Have you ever walked away from an argument with your husband feeling more wounded than heard? Or repeated a cycle of conflict that leaves both of you exhausted and distant? It's not always because the other person is the problem. Sometimes, it's because you're aiming your weapons in the wrong direction. In spiritual warfare, and especially in marriage, misidentifying the enemy is one of the enemy's greatest tactics. When you make your spouse the target, you take your eyes off the real source of division: the adversary of your soul and the destroyer of godly unions.

Satan hates unity. He hates any relationship that reflects God's love and design, and marriage does both. That's why he works overtime to put husband and wife against each other.

If you don't identify this spiritual reality, you'll:

- Fight your husband instead of fighting for him.
- Use natural weapons instead of spiritual ones.
- View every disagreement as a personal attack instead of a potential strategy session.

When You Ask, God Will Show You the Enemy

We don't just need prayer; we need prophetic clarity. We don't just need to rebuke; we need to reveal and remove what's behind the scenes. I remember a time when my son used to wake up every night at about 2 a.m. screaming from nightmares. I prayed. I anointed. I rebuked. And yet, the pattern continued. Night after night, it felt like torment had taken residence in my home. And my baby was paying the price.

One night, I was fed up. I was tired of praying powerless prayers. I said out loud, "This has to stop now! I'm sick and tired of this!" After getting my son settled again, I laid down in my bed and said something simple but life-altering: "God, show me what's really happening." Immediately, I saw a vision. Someone was standing outside my back gate, looking directly at my son's window. Dressed in black from head to toe, with a solid black mask like a demonic version of Spider-Man. I don't know if it was a person or a creature. But it was real. And it had been assigned. The Holy Spirit said, "He's going to cry again." And sure enough, he did. But this time, his words pierced the air: "The spiders are chasing me!" I ran into his room, not with fear, but with spiritual fire. I stood by that window, and I spoke directly to the thing I saw.

"You will leave and never come back! I destroy your power and influence off my son and my family. I send you to hell

34

in Jesus' name! From this day, you are no longer a problem in my life!"

That was it! No more 2 a.m. cries. No more night terrors. No more torment. Because I stopped fighting blindly. I asked God to reveal the real enemy to me, and I dealt with him.

I didn't know it at the time, but even that prayer, raw and desperate, was a form of surrender. I wasn't trying to be right. I wasn't even thinking about having a pure heart. I was simply tired, and I needed God to step in. But now, looking back, I see it clearly: there's a kind of clarity that only comes when the heart is postured toward Heaven. Not perfect but postured. Not without emotion but willing to yield. The Bible says, "Blessed are the pure in heart, for they shall see God." (Matthew 5:8, ESV). Sometimes, that *seeing* isn't a vision in the clouds. It's seeing what's really going on behind the chaos. It's seeing what's spiritual when everything around you feel emotional. It's when God gives you eyes to spot the snake before it strikes. I believe that's what happened that night. I didn't have it all together, but I had a heart turned toward God. And He honored that.

Here's the part I don't want you to miss: the same God who exposed the enemy standing at my son's window is the same God who wants to expose the hidden enemies standing at the window of your marriage. Maybe your home has been tense. Maybe arguments keep circling the same unresolved mountain. Maybe your heart feels tired, stretched, or even numb. And maybe—just maybe—you've been fighting hard but in the wrong direction. There are moments when you can't sleep, not because of noise but because of the unrest in your spirit. You lie awake under the weight of disagreement, confusion, emotional distance, and burdens you can't quite name. And God is inviting you to do the same thing I did, ask Him to show you what's really happening.

The holy fire that rose up in me that night wasn't just for my child. It's the same kind of fire God wants to stir in you for your marriage. A fire that refuses to accept cycles of division as normal. A fire that gets fed up with confusion and declares in the Spirit: "This must stop. Father, show me what's really going on. Teach me how to pray".

Holy Anger is not Sin—It's Strategy

Sometimes, your anger isn't wrong. It just needs to be aimed properly. I wasn't mad at my son. I was angry at the presence behind the pattern. Dysfunction is not normal. Torment is not normal. And you must refuse to become comfortable with patterns that erode your peace. The enemy loves when you're passive. He thrives on your acceptance of chaos. But when you rise in holy fire and say, "Enough is enough," you shift from surviving to warring with wisdom.

Enemy Tactics in Marriage

Like any strategic opponent, the enemy doesn't always attack with obvious weapons. His approach is often subtle, targeted, and psychological. Here are some common spiritual warfare tactics used to divide marriages:

1. *Division by Offense*
   A misheard tone. A misunderstood comment. A memory replayed with suspicion.

   "He doesn't care."
   "She's always like this."

   Offense always festers where grace should dwell.

2. *Isolation by Silence*
   The enemy thrives in disconnection. He'll whisper, "Why bother trying?" and encourage avoidance over engagement.

3. *Distraction by Busyness*
   Ministry. Work. Kids. Life. When connection becomes transactional, intimacy dies quietly.

4. *Comparison as a Poison*
   He'll make you question your worth or your spouse's adequacy by planting envy or idealized images of other marriages.

Discernment vs. Division

Discernment allows you to see through the moment and into the mission. It is the Holy Spirit causing you to see rightly when your natural eyes want to accuse.

Discernment says:
"What's really going on here?"
"What lie might I be believing right now?"
"What does God's Word say about this situation?"

Division says:
"He's never going to change."
"I'll just protect myself."
"What's the point of even trying?"

Misunderstanding the Mission: Lessons from Moses and Jesus

I can't stress enough how important it is to recognize who the real enemy is. Let's reflect on the story of *Moses and the Israelites*. Every time they were frustrated or felt God was delaying, they attacked Moses. Their grumbling caused Moses to grow weary, and in his frustration, he misrepresented God. Though he was simply trying to lead them into the promise, their rebellion hindered his mission. As wives, we often misplace our frustration, turning our husbands into enemies when they're really co-laborers in our call. Instead of holding up their hands in the heat of battle like Aaron and Hur did for Moses in the middle of a war (Exodus 17:12), we tear them down. And as a result, the whole household suffers.

Now look at *Jesus*, the Groom of all grooms. As He was heading to the cross to save us, to redeem His bride, it was the very people He came to redeem who were attacking Him. They spat on Him, mocked Him, and crucified Him, yet He still pursued the mission… This is a moment to pause and thank God He is not like man! Let us not crucify our husbands out of misidentification. He is not your enemy. He is the one you were called to help as you both pursue the promise together.

To the Wife Whose Husband is Not Yet Saved

Let me minister to the wife whose husband is not yet saved: your husband is not your enemy. You have a responsibility not to fix him, not to shame him, but to pray for him, cover him, and remain lovable before him. The Bible says, "Husbands, love your wives, as Christ loved the church and gave himself up for her" (Ephesians 5:25, ESV). But here's a truth you need to hear: your husband may not come to church because he loves Christ. He may come because he loves you. That means your life must reflect

Christ so well that he becomes curious, then convicted by the Holy Spirit, and eventually converted.

Jesus said, "This is my commandment, that you love one another as I have loved you" (John 15:12, ESV). So even though your husband may not yet believe or attend church, you still have a divine mandate: to be faithful, committed, gracious, merciful, kind, and yes—submissive. Every instruction the Word gives to wives still applies. Your obedience could be the seed that shifts his eternity. As Paul wrote, "For the unbelieving husband has been sanctified through his wife, and the unbelieving wife has been sanctified through her believing husband" (1 Corinthians 7:14, NIV). This means your presence and obedience has a sanctifying influence in your home.

I remember when I first got saved, and my husband wasn't saved yet. I would invite him to church, and often, he was just too tired to come. I used to get disappointed and say things to guilt him. One day, my cousin gently corrected me: "Don't do that. Just keep inviting him. If he comes, he comes. If not, that's okay. But don't make him feel bad." I took that advice to heart. I kept praying for him. I stopped complaining so much and started loving on him more. I remember once, one of my husband's friend's wives asked, "Your wife doesn't have a problem with you going out all the time?" But the Holy Spirit was helping me to become more understanding. I never stopped praying for my husband. Every time there was an altar call, I silently interceded.

One year later, my husband walked down the aisle and said yes to Christ, and God slowly began to shift his rhythm. My husband didn't accept Christ at first because he loved Him. He did it because he loved me. Over time, he came to see that the love I showed him daily, unconditional, steadfast, and enduring, was really the love of Christ. Eventually, he said yes to the love of Christ for himself. The Holy Spirit taught me how to remain lovable by becoming a vessel of Love Himself. Today, one of the most beautiful things to behold is my husband's love and reverence for Christ.

I remember one year during a church conference when my current pastor, Pastor Travis Haynes, was the guest speaker. My husband came that night straight from work, and though he wasn't yet saved, Pastor prophesied to him. He declared that the Lord was going to use my husband mightily in the Kingdom, that God would manifest Himself through him, and that he would do great work for the Lord. In that moment, someone had to quickly take baby Nala from my arms because I fell out glorifying God. Even though my husband wasn't saved yet, I knew God had already answered my prayers. Pastor Travis didn't say, 'The Lord is going to save you.' He spoke purpose. He spoke destiny. And in that moment, God whispered to my spirit, 'He is Mine.'

From then on, my prayers shifted. I no longer prayed from desperation, but from gratitude: 'God, I thank You that You've saved him. I thank You for the work You will do through him. I thank You for how You'll advance the Kingdom through his life.' Six months later, my husband walked down the aisle and received the life of Christ.

Today, my husband is an Ordained Deacon in the Lord's Church, affirmed by the very pastor who prophesied that word over him ten years earlier — the same man who is now our current pastor. That is how faithful God is.

This is my encouragement to you: be lovable, woman of God. Your husband is not your enemy. Pray for him to recognize, acknowledge, and receive God's love. Remember, as Romans 2:4 says, it is the kindness of God that leads us to repentance. Trust the Holy Spirit to do the rest.

Once you've identified the real enemy, you can stop wasting energy on the wrong battles and start waging war where it matters most: in prayer. We'll dive into that in the next chapter.

Prayer

Father, thank You for trusting me with this marriage. I lift my husband before You. You know him by name. You see every part of his heart, and You love him more than I ever could. I pray that You would draw him gently to Yourself. Soften his heart to Your Spirit. Let him see Jesus through my life. Help me to remain faithful, gentle, and loving even when it's hard. Teach me to reflect Your grace without nagging, shaming, or pushing. Give me the strength to love like You love, steadfast, sacrificial, and pure. And God... purify my heart. I don't always see clearly. I don't always respond gently. But I want to. So, remove what's fogging my vision. Wash my heart so that I can see You in my husband, in my home, and in the heat of the battle. Let me be the kind of wife who helps him hear Your call. In Jesus' name, Amen.

Journal Reflection

Reflect on what God is speaking to you right now.

Lord, where have I been seeing through offense instead of purity?

Where are You inviting me to pause and ask for Your perspective?

Am I making my husband the enemy, or am I asking You to help me see with clarity?

Scripture Meditation:

Take time to write these out and ask God to make them personal in this season:

- Matthew 5:8 (ESV): "Blessed are the pure in heart, for they shall see God."

- 1 Peter 3:1-2 (ESV): "Likewise, wives, be subject to your own husbands, so that even if some do not obey the word, they may be won without a word by the conduct of their wives—when they see your respectful and pure conduct."
- Galatians 6:9 (ESV): "And let us not grow weary of doing good, for in due season we will reap, if we do not give up."

- Romans 12:12 (ESV): "Rejoice in hope, be patient in tribulation, be constant in prayer.

FIVE

THE WAR ROOM: STRATEGIC PRAYER PLANNING

Every Victory Starts in the War Room

In military terms, no general begins a battle without a strategy. The war is not won in the noise of combat but in the silence of the strategy room. In the Kingdom of God, that war room is prayer. It's not your last resort; it's your first move. Your war room is where Heaven meets Earth. It's where divine insight is released. Where God gives you keys to unlock answers, overturn attacks, and shift spiritual climates before they manifest in the natural.

As a wife, you are not just holding a family together. You are holding a frontline post in a spiritual war. And your weapons are not carnal, they are mighty through God (2 Corinthians 10:4, KJV). Prayer is not the side dish of your spiritual walk. It is the war map, the battle cry, and the lifeline. So, if you're going to win in your marriage, you must learn to fight first in secret.

Prayer Moves Heaven and Confronts Hell

Prayer is not emotional venting. It's not repetitive words said out of habit. It is conversation with your Father in Heaven, who is the Commander-in-Chief of Heaven's armies. It is you coming in agreement with what He has already done for you. It is where the weakest woman can become the most dangerous to darkness. You don't need perfect words; you need persistent presence.

A praying wife:

- Shifts the spiritual climate of her home
- Covers her family's identity and destiny
- Gains clarity in confusion
- Invites divine intervention where her hands can't reach

Yes, there are times when prayer is quiet. But never confuse quietness with weakness. God moves powerfully, not because we speak loudly, but because He listens and answers. Effective prayer is rooted in truth, faith, obedience, and intimacy. You don't have to shout to see God working it out for you. His working it out for you is not different from his will being done. The things we ask God to do in prayer shouldn't be different from the plans he already has for us. That's why prayer should be a two-way conversation. It's the place where God shows us His heart concerning our lives.

Praying in the Name of Jesus — This is not a Tagline

Many people pray "in the name of Jesus" without understanding the meaning of what they're saying. It's not a magical phrase or a password that forces Heaven's hand. It's a legal access point that comes through covenant. To pray "in the name of Jesus" means to come under His authority, to stand in His identity, and to speak as one who is in covenant with Him. The Greek word for "name" in this context is *onoma*, which refers not just to a title but to the essence, character, and reputation of a person. When you pray in Jesus' name, you are praying as one who belongs to Him, as a daughter who has access to the Father because you are in Christ. We don't come to God in our own righteousness. We come because we are hidden in the One who is always righteous, always obedient, and always heard. That's why Jesus said: "Whatever you ask in My name, this I will do, that the Father may be glorified in the Son." — John 14:13 (ESV).

Praying in His name is not about manipulating results. It's about aligning with His will, walking in His delegated authority, and trusting His unchanging character. You don't have to perform to be heard. You simply have to be positioned in Him.

Worship That Wins — A Worshipping Wife is a Winning Wife

When I first came to Christ, I didn't fully understand what it meant to worship, truly worship. I would sit in services and see people around me falling out in the Spirit, tears flowing, hands lifted high. If I'm honest, I would wonder if I really loved God at all, because I didn't feel what they felt. I didn't cry the way they cried. I didn't fall or have goosebumps or shout in awe. At some point, I began to feel like a hypocrite. I was repeating the right words—I heard others say them. But those words didn't connect with my heart. They felt like empty phrases, like echoes of other people's experiences that I hadn't personally lived. I started questioning, "Do I really love God? Am I just pretending?" And then one day, in the stillness, God whispered something that forever changed me: "You have to let Me love you first." He continued, "You won't be able to truly worship Me until you learn to love Me. And you won't be able to truly love Me until you learn how to receive My love first."

That moment marked the beginning of a sacred journey with the Holy Spirit. He brought me into the real war room, not just a physical space, but a spiritual posture, where He re-taught me many things I thought I knew. He taught me to stop praying like others and start praying like me. He would stop me mid-prayer and ask, "What does that mean?" I realized I had been saying things I didn't even understand. He would lead me into Scripture, not from ritual, but from relationship. Not to pull a verse at random, but to seek truth that matched the word He was already whispering to my heart. It was in that place I truly met Him. Not through formulas, but through fellowship. I learned to stop performing and start receiving. I learned to recognize Him in the ordinary moments of my life and in every experience, whether good or bad. Worship stopped being a ritual and became my response.

Now, when I pray, it's not about sounding powerful; it's about being present. It's not about quoting Scripture to prove my faith. It's about receiving the Rhema that fuels it.

God is not calling you to become a powerful prayer warrior. You are a woman who serves and prays to a powerful God who answers prayers. This powerful God lives in you, is with you, and He is your Father. This posture keeps us humble and surrendered. God is not looking for perfection; He's looking for honesty. He wants to meet you in that secret place. He wants to correct how you view worship, prayer, yourself, and Him. You don't have to mimic anyone else. Your authentic voice, your real heart, and your willingness to receive His love are more than enough. He'll meet you in your doubt and your desires, and in this place, you'll realize that His desires have become yours, which includes a healthy and prosperous marriage and family.

Fighting from the Shelter of Who He Is

Before you ever open your mouth in spiritual warfare, remember this: you don't fight for victory, you fight from it. Your strength doesn't come from your posture, your knowledge, or even your prayer routine. It comes from the God who covers, surrounds, and fights for you. The war room is not just where you speak. It's where you hide. It's where you anchor yourself in the identity of the One who has never lost a battle.

In moments of fear, resistance, or frustration, you don't need to feel strong, you need to run to the Strong One. Below are names of God that reveal who He is in battle. As a wife, you can call on these names and know that you are secured under His covering. These names are not just titles. They are weapons. They are shelters. They are truths you can rest in when the enemy wants you to be reactive, weary, or feel unprotected.

Jehovah Sabaoth – The Lord of Hosts
The Commander of Heaven's Armies. He leads every battle, including yours. "Who is this King of glory? The Lord of hosts, he is the King of glory!" (Psalm 24:10, ESV)

El Gibbor – Mighty God
Your divine warrior. There is no battle He cannot win. "For to us a child is born... and his name shall be called Wonderful Counselor, Mighty God, Everlasting Father, Prince of Peace." (Isaiah 9:6, ESV)

Jehovah Nissi – The Lord Is My Banner
He is the flag over your house. You march under His name, not your own. "And Moses built an altar and called the name of it, The Lord is My Banner." (Exodus 17:15, ESV)

Jehovah Maginnenu – Our Shield
He blocks every flaming arrow of accusation and fear. Psalm 3:3 (ESV) – "But you, O Lord, are a shield about me, my glory, and the lifter of my head."

Moshia – Deliverer / Savior
The one who pulls you out. No pit is too deep. "The Lord is my rock and my fortress and my deliverer, my God, my rock, in whom I take refuge, my shield, and the horn of my salvation, my stronghold." (Psalm 18:2, ESV)

Yahweh Shammah – The Lord Is There
He is present in every silent cry and every closed-door battle. "And the name of the city from that time on shall be, The Lord Is There." (Ezekiel 48:35, ESV)

Yahweh Tsuri – The Lord Is my Rock
Stable. Immovable. Unshakable. That's the foundation you fight from. "The Lord is my rock and my fortress and my deliverer, my God, my rock, in whom I take refuge..." (Psalm 18:2, ESV)

Go'el – Redeemer / Avenger of Blood
The one who defends what belongs to Him and restores what was lost. "Their Redeemer is strong; the Lord of hosts is his name. He will surely plead their cause." (Jeremiah 50:34, ESV)

El Roi – The God Who Sees Me
He sees the unseen battles, the misunderstood moments, and the weight you carry. "So she called the name of the Lord who spoke to her, 'You are a God of seeing,' for she said, 'Truly here I have seen him who looks after me." (Genesis 16:13, ESV)

Yahweh Elohe Yisrael – The Lord, the God of Israel
The covenant-keeping God who defends His people. You are included. "Blessed be the Lord, the God of Israel, who alone does wondrous things." (Psalm 72:18, ESV)

Reflection & Activation
- Which name speaks to the battle you're in right now?
- Speak it aloud. Write it on your wall. Whisper it when you don't have the strength to pray.

You don't fight alone. You don't fight uncovered. You fight from the shelter of His name.

Strategic Intercession and Elijah: Power in the Private Place

Before Elijah ever stood on Mount Carmel and called down fire from Heaven, he stood in the war room, the secret place. James 5:17–18 (ESV) reminds us:

> "Elijah was a man with a nature like ours, and he prayed fervently that it might not rain, and for three years and six months it did not rain on the earth. Then he prayed again, and heaven gave rain, and the earth bore its fruit."

Elijah was a man of prayer. He didn't gain authority in public because of charisma. He received it in private. When he challenged the prophets of Baal, he wasn't operating in spontaneity (1 Kings 18:20-40). He had already received a Word from God and instructions for how to proceed. His confidence didn't come from volume or performance, it came from knowing Heaven had already answered. This is the fruit of the war room. Intimacy builds trust in God. Elijah didn't pray on the mountaintop, hoping something would happen. He had already been in conversation with the Commander-in-Chief.

When you pray like Elijah, you don't just talk; you listen. You don't just react; you receive. You get instructions, timing, insight, and clarity. God still answers by fire. But the fire doesn't fall for performance; it falls in response to alignment.

Prayer Strategy Template

Every military leader needs a strategy. Here's a simple structure you can adapt that is in alignment with God's blueprint for our lives:

1. Worship — Open with praise and thanksgiving. Worship shifts your posture from fear to faith. Worship God for who He is. Worship Him from where you are, based on who you know Him to be. Reflect on your past experiences and interactions with Him. How did He reveal Himself to you?

2. Confess and Surrender — Invite God to search your heart. When you are in this posture, God will reveal His heart to you concerning your family.

PRAY FOR YOUR HUSBAND

His Relationship with God (Spiritual Leadership)
- That he would love God with all his heart, soul, and strength
- That he would hear God clearly and follow His voice
- That he would hunger for the Word and walk in truth
- That his identity would be anchored in Christ, not culture, status, or performance
- That he would be submitted to Christ, as Christ is to the Father
- (Mark 12:30, John 10:27, Psalm 1:2–3, Ephesians 2:10, 1 Corinthians 11:3)

His Role as Head of the Home (Covering & Governance)

- That he would walk in humility, wisdom, and courage as he leads
- That he would govern the household with justice and mercy
- That he would cover his wife and children in prayer and presence
- That he would make decisions led by the Spirit, not pressure or pride
- That he would not shrink back from responsibility, even in weariness
- That he would cherish his wife in love, intimacy, and tenderness
- That his affection and faithfulness would strengthen the covenant of marriage
- That no counterfeit desire or outside influence would break the bond
- (James 3:17, Micah 6:8, Ephesians 5:25–28, Proverbs 3:5–6, Galatians 6:9 1 Corinthians 7:3–5, Proverbs 5:18–19)

His Role as Protector

- That God would place divine discernment in his spirit to recognize and resist spiritual attacks
- That he would be sensitive to the atmosphere of the home and guard its peace
- That he would protect the hearts of his wife and children through love, time, and intentionality
- That he would not be passive in conflict but vigilant in spiritual warfare
- (1 Peter 5:8, Isaiah 32:18, 1 Corinthians 13:7, Ephesians 6:10–12)

His Role as Provider
- That God would bless the work of his hands and open doors for provision
- That his heart would be content and not tormented by comparison or lack
- That he would steward finances wisely, generously, and with integrity
- That God would surround him with divine connections, mentors, and opportunities
- That his work and reputation would reflect Christ to those around him
- That his integrity in business and community would bring honor to God
- That his workplace would become a field of influence for the Kingdom
- (Deuteronomy 28:12, Philippians 4:11–13, Proverbs 13:11, Proverbs 11:14 Colossians 3:23, Matthew 5:16, Proverbs 22:1)

His Mental and Emotional Health
- That he would be honest about his struggles and find safe places to process
- That he would not carry silent pressure but release it to God
- That shame, fear, or failure would not define him
- That joy, peace, and clarity would replace confusion and heaviness
- That he would find rest and renewal in God's presence, not strive from emptiness
- That the Lord would teach him rhythms of sabbath and stillness
- That joy and strength would be restored as he learns to abide in Christ

- (Galatians 6:2, Matthew 11:28-29, Romans 8:1, Isaiah 61:3 Psalm 127:2, Isaiah 40:31)

His Physical Health and Strength
- That he would walk in divine health and strength all his days
- That sickness, disease, and generational infirmities would be cut off from him
- That God would heal every place of weakness and restore vitality
- That his body would be protected from premature aging, accidents, and affliction
- That he would prosper in health as his soul prospers (Exodus 15:26, Isaiah 53:5, 3 John 1:2, Psalm 91:9–10, Psalm 121:7)

His Relationships and Accountability
- That God would surround him with godly friends who sharpen and encourage him
- That he would have healthy accountability, free from pride and secrecy
- That he would flee from temptation and walk in purity
- That he would honor and cherish his covenant with you
- (Proverbs 27:17, James 5:16, 1 Corinthians 10:13, Malachi 2:15)

His Legacy and Kingdom Impact
- That he would disciple his children by example, not just words
- That his life would reflect the love, power, and consistency of Christ

- That God would activate him to build generational blessing, not just provision
- That his purpose would be fulfilled
- (Deuteronomy 6:6–7, 2 Corinthians 3:2–3, Psalm 112:1–2, Acts 13:36)

PRAY FOR YOUR CHILDREN

Their Salvation and Spiritual Identity
- That they would know Jesus early and love Him deeply
- That they would be secure in their identity as sons and daughters of God
- That they would walk in the Spirit and not be ruled by the flesh
- That their hearts would be tender and receptive to God's voice
- (Matthew 19:14, Romans 8:14–16, Galatians 5:16–17, 3 John 1:4)

Their Purpose and Kingdom Assignment
- That they would discover and walk in the purpose for which they were born
- That their gifts would be nurtured and used for God's glory
- That they would not chase success but fulfill divine assignment
- That they would carry a burden for souls and the advancement of God's Kingdom
- That they would be filled with the Holy Spirit and operate in His gifts
- That prophecy, discernment, wisdom, and boldness would mark their lives

- That they would recognize their spiritual gifts early and use them for God's glory
- (Jeremiah 1:5, Ephesians 2:10, Acts 20:24, Matthew 28:19–20, Joel 2:28, 1 Corinthians 12:7–11, Acts 2:17–18)

Their Emotional and Mental Health
- That fear, anxiety, and insecurity would not take root in their hearts
- That joy, confidence, and peace would be their portion
- That they would learn healthy expression and emotional resilience
- That they would be covered from trauma, shame, and self-hatred
- (2 Timothy 1:7, Isaiah 61:3, Philippians 4:6–7, Psalm 34:4–5)

Their Physical Health and Healing
- That they would walk in health and strength all their days
- That sickness, disease, and generational infirmities would be cut off from their lives
- That they would experience God as their Healer in every season
- That no affliction or premature death would come near them
- (Exodus 15:26, Isaiah 53:5, Jeremiah 30:17, 3 John 1:2)

Their Protection and Discernment
- That God would shield them from spiritual, physical, and relational harm
- That they would recognize danger and flee temptation
- That they would be sensitive to spiritual atmospheres
- That angels would guard their coming in and going out

- (Psalm 91:11, 1 Peter 5:8, Proverbs 4:23, Psalm 121:7–8)

Their Obedience and Teachability
- That they would honor authority and walk in humility
- That they would have a teachable spirit and love instruction
- That their hearts would not harden in rebellion or pride
- That they would value correction as a form of love and safety
- (Ephesians 6:1–3, Proverbs 13:1, Hebrews 12:11, Proverbs 12:1)

Their Friendships and Influences
- That God would connect them with godly, purpose-aligned peers
- That they would be protected from toxic relationships and peer pressure
- That they would have boldness to stand for righteousness
- That they would influence others toward Christ
- (Proverbs 13:20, 1 Corinthians 15:33, 2 Timothy 2:22, Matthew 5:16)

Their Appetite for God's Word and Presence
- That they would love the Bible and understand spiritual truths
- That prayer and worship would become natural rhythms in their life
- That they would encounter the Holy Spirit personally
- That they would not be satisfied with religion, but long for God
- (Psalm 119:105, Matthew 5:6, John 10:27, Psalm 42:1–2)

Their Future Spouse and Covenant Marriage
- That their future spouse would be growing in grace, purity, and purpose
- That they would be kept from emotional entanglements and premature intimacy
- That they would be prepared to love, honor, and serve in covenant
- That they would be sensitive to what God ordained and His divine alignment and holy timing
- (Proverbs 18:22, 2 Corinthians 6:14, Song of Songs 8:4, Malachi 2:15)

Their Academic and Intellectual Development
- That they would learn with joy, curiosity, and focus
- That God would give them wisdom beyond their age
- That they would be diligent and disciplined in their studies
- That they would see education as a tool for purpose, not pressure
- (Daniel 1:17, Proverbs 4:7, Ecclesiastes 9:10, Colossians 3:23–24)

Their Legacy and Generational Impact
- That they would build upon your prayers, not repeat generational cycles
- That their lives would bear fruit that lasts for eternity
- That they would disciple others and multiply righteousness
- That they would be arrows of light sent into darkness with purpose and power
- (Psalm 112:1–2, Isaiah 61:9, Psalm 127:3–5, Matthew 5:14–16)

PRAY FOR YOURSELF

Your Intimacy with God
- That you would hunger for God's presence more than platforms or performance
- That your identity would be rooted in who God says you are, not what you do
- That you would hear His voice clearly and walk in step with the Spirit
- That you would be refreshed daily and abide in Christ as your source
- (Psalm 27:4, John 15:4–5, Romans 8:14, Isaiah 40:31)

Your Role as a Wife
- That you would honor your husband even when it's hard, and trust God with the results
- That your words would bring life, wisdom, and healing into your home
- That you would be both strong and surrendered in your posture
- That your love would be patient, kind, and rooted in truth
- That you would walk in wisdom and spiritual sensitivity to help your husband reach his next level
- (Proverbs 14:1, Ephesians 5:22–24, 1 Peter 3:1–4, 1 Corinthians 13:4–7, Ecclesiastes 4:9–10)

Your Role as a Mother
- That you would see your children not as interruptions but as assignments
- That you would partner with the Holy Spirit to raise your children according to Heaven's original design for their lives

- That God would give you discernment to see beyond behavior into their hearts
- That your discipline would be anchored in love, not frustration
- That you would be a safe place for their growth, questions, and mistakes
- (Psalm 127:3–5, John 16:13, ESV, Proverbs 22:6, Deuteronomy 6:6–7, Isaiah 54:13)

Your Emotional and Mental Health

- That peace would guard your heart and mind in Christ Jesus
- That you would reject shame, guilt, and burnout as badges of worth
- That your joy would be renewed, even in routine and repetition
- That you would know when to pause, ask for help, and rest
- (Philippians 4:6–7, Romans 8:1, Nehemiah 8:10, Matthew 11:28–30)

Your Physical Health and Strength

- That you would walk in health, energy, and strength to fulfill your calling
- That sickness, disease, and generational infirmities would be broken off your body
- That you would care for your body as the temple of the Holy Spirit
- That you would experience renewal, healing, and longevity in every season
- (3 John 1:2, Psalm 103:2–3, Proverbs 31:17, 1 Corinthians 6:19–20)

Your Spiritual Warfare and Discernment
- That you would not war against people but against the real enemy
- That your prayers would be Spirit-led, not fear-driven
- That you would discern patterns, strongholds, and spiritual assignments
- That you would guard the gates of your home with holy boldness
- (2 Corinthians 10:3–5, Ephesians 6:10–13, Proverbs 4:23, Luke 10:19)

Your Stewardship and Priorities
- That you would manage your time and home with wisdom and grace
- That you would not compare your pace or calling to others
- That you would choose what is necessary over what is merely urgent
- That you would be faithful in the little, trusting God with the much
- (Proverbs 31:27, Colossians 3:23–24, Luke 16:10, Psalm 90:12)

Your Relationships and Community
- That God would place you in covenant friendships that uplift and sharpen
- That you would not suffer in silence but walk in truth and transparency
- That you would forgive quickly and love freely
- That your heart would remain tender, even after disappointment
- (Ecclesiastes 4:9–10, James 5:16, Colossians 3:13–14, Proverbs 27:9)

Your Calling and Spiritual Gifts
- That you would boldly steward the gifts God has placed in you
- That fear, insecurity, and comparison would not silence your anointing
- That you would fan into flame every gift of the Spirit entrusted to you
- That your calling would advance God's Kingdom and leave an eternal impact
- (1 Peter 4:10–11, 2 Timothy 1:6–7, Romans 12:6–8, Acts 1:8)

Your Legacy and Eternal Focus
- That your obedience today would plant seeds for generations
- That your private life would reflect the same grace as your public life
- That you would raise your children with eternity in view, not survival
- That Heaven would recognize your faith, even when the world doesn't
- (2 Timothy 1:5, Matthew 6:33, Hebrews 12:1–2, Galatians 6:9)

Handling Opposition Through Prayer and Truth

When we war in prayer, the focus is not on the enemy. It's on the unshakable truth of what God has already done for us. Jesus taught us to love our enemies and pray for those who persecute us (Matthew 5:44), and we are also called to stand firm against the spiritual forces of darkness (Ephesians 6:12). There are certain scriptures I return to often when I sense resistance in the spirit. I love the Psalms; I believe we all do. But even more, I anchor myself in these truths:

- "If God is for us, who can be against us?" (Romans 8:31, ESV)
- "We are more than conquerors through Him who loved us." (Romans 8:37, ESV)
- "He who is in you is greater than he who is in the world." (1 John 4:4, ESV)
- "Those who are with us are more than those who are with them." (2 Kings 6:16, ESV)
- "You prepare a table before me in the presence of my enemies." (Psalm 23:5, ESV)

When the enemy feels close, don't shrink back. Remember the table. If the enemy is near, it means God is near too, preparing something for you. What was meant to harm becomes a moment of honor. What looked like warfare becomes the setup for a feast.

Don't forget the real enemy. Sometimes the adversary uses people, especially those who are weary, wounded, or unaware of how open they've become. But people are not the real problem. If we stay distracted fighting the vessel, we'll miss the spirit behind it. "For we do not wrestle against flesh and blood, but against the rulers, against the authorities, against the cosmic powers over this present darkness, against the spiritual forces of evil in the heavenly places." (Ephesians 6:12, ESV).

Offense is a decoy that delays your discernment. Attacking the person may satisfy your emotions in the moment, but it won't shut down the source. When we go to God and war in the Spirit, the enemy's assignment is dismantled at the root. And often, the very person the enemy tried to use may have a chance to be set free, because we chose obedience over reaction.

David's Posture in the War Room

When I think about the war room and prayer, David stands out as a model of how to posture our hearts amid conflict. David was pursued by enemies, betrayed by people he trusted, and hunted by Saul himself. Yet what marks David's life is not the chaos around him, but the direction of his heart. His posture was always toward God.

David teaches us something powerful: it is safer to take our anger, frustration, and even harsh words to God than to unleash them on people. Again and again in the Psalms, we see David crying out, "The trouble they cause recoils on them; their violence comes down on their own heads " (Psalm 7:16, NIV) or "Break the arm of the wicked man; call the evildoer to account for his wickedness" (Psalm 10:15, NIV). Those words sound sharp, but notice where he spoke them: before God. David trusted that God could handle the weight of his emotions, filter his words through mercy, and respond with justice that was right and true.

This is a safe place for us, too. When those we care about come against us, when we feel betrayed or attacked, our instinct is often to fight back in the flesh. But David shows us another way. He turned his frustrations toward God. He was honest. He was transparent. And even in his raw cries for vengeance, we often see him soften into repentance, declaring his trust in God's faithfulness:

"Oh that you would slay the wicked, O God! O men of blood, depart from me! They speak against you with malicious intent; your enemies take your name in vain. Do I not hate those who hate you, O Lord? And do I not loathe those who rise up against you? I hate them with complete hatred; I count them my enemies. Search me, O God, and know my heart! Try me and know my thoughts! And see if there be any grievous way in me, and lead me in the way everlasting!" (Psalm 139:19–24, ESV).

This is what it means to fight in the war room. It is not pretending we are not angry or hurt. It is choosing to bring all of it—our tears, our rage, our confusion before God instead of against people. When we do this, we give God the room to be our defender. And we position ourselves not in the chaos of offense, but in the safety of His presence.

I encourage you: let the Holy Spirit guide your warfare. Use the Word. Pray boldly. And instead of praying for people to be harmed, target the demonic systems, mindsets, and strongholds at work. Ask God to intervene, to overtake minds, to bring conviction and mercy. That's how victory looks in the Kingdom. Remember, we don't pray for victory, we pray from victory. Jesus already won. We just need to partner with what He's already done for us.

Let your prayer room become a training ground for generational intercession. Don't just pray about problems, pray with prophetic authority. Your consistency in the secret place builds confidence in your children and courage in your husband. You are a gatekeeper. Stand strong.

Praying Without Bias

Let me give you some advice for when you're praying for your husband, especially in moments of conflict. There's something the Holy Spirit taught me. When I go into God's presence, particularly after a disagreement, I step outside of my role as 'wife'. I don't want my emotions or frustrations to cloud what God wants to reveal to me.

So, I say, "Father, I've come to talk to You about Your son."

This posture is a true moment of surrender. It allows me to see my husband the way God sees him. Through mercy, purpose, and love. And it allows God to show me myself, my blind spots, my assumptions, and where I may have contributed to the breakdown. Sometimes, it's not just your husband that needs to change. Sometimes, it's you. Or maybe he's just a son of God who's wrestling, and what he really needs is a sister in the spirit, not a wife with a list. When God restores His son, your husband will rise. So come to Him without an agenda. Come as a covenant partner standing in the gap, not a judge making accusations. God honors that posture.

Strategic Prayer & Victory: From Revelation to Obedience

Prayer is not the end of the battle, it's the beginning of your assignment. What happens in the war room is sacred, but what happens after the war room is what seals the victory. Many of us cry out to God, hear clearly, and feel peace, but then stop short of obedience. We walk away from prayer encouraged, but we often fail to follow through. We don't build the ark. We don't march around the wall. We don't show up on the battlefield. But Kingdom strategy doesn't stop at hearing. It demands doing. Jehoshaphat is a perfect example of this. He didn't just pray, he followed through on every detail God gave him.

In 2 Chronicles 20, Jehoshaphat, king of Judah, was faced with a vast army made up of three enemy nations: the Moabites, Ammonites, and Meunites. Overwhelmed and outnumbered, he did not first prepare his soldiers. Instead, the Bible says, "Jehoshaphat was afraid and set his face to seek the Lord" (2 Chronicles 20:3, ESV). He called the entire nation to fast and pray, and as they sought God together, the Spirit of the Lord came upon Jahaziel with a prophetic word: "Do not be afraid and do not be dismayed at this great horde, for the battle is not yours but God's" (2 Chronicles 20:15, ESV).

God gave them a specific strategy:

1. Do not fear.
2. Go out and face the enemy.
3. Put the worshippers at the front.
4. Sing praises to the Lord.

They obeyed exactly as God instructed. And when the worshippers began to sing and praise, the Lord caused the enemy armies to turn on each other and destroy themselves. Judah never had to draw a sword. Their victory was won in obedience to God's instruction in prayer. "And when they began to sing and praise, the Lord set an ambush against the men... who had come against Judah, so that they were routed" (2 Chronicles 20:22, ESV).

The key? Jehoshaphat didn't just pray, he followed through. He carried out what God gave him in the war room. That is where the victory was sealed. Don't just pray. Do what is required of you. Many times, our issue is not that we don't pray; the problem is we don't follow instructions.

Remain pure in prayer. When your motives are pure, your spiritual vision sharpens. You see your husband not just as he is but as God sees him. You see your children with discernment. You see strategies with precision. Ask God to purify your heart daily, not to become impressive in prayer, but to become intimate. The war room belongs to those who see, and those who see clearly are the ones who come with clean hands and a pure heart. Let your prayers flow from that place, and you will experience the fullness of what God desires to reveal.

Let this chapter mark a shift, not just in how you pray, but in how you listen, follow, and lead. In the next chapter, we'll uncover the divine chain of command that governs every Kingdom home.

Prayer

Father, I thank You for the man You've entrusted to me. I lift up my husband before You. Strengthen him in his inner being. Guard his heart, renew his mind, and align his desires with Yours. I speak peace over his thoughts, protection over his path, and joy into his spirit. May he lead with wisdom, love with purity, and walk in obedience to Your will. Where he feels weak, be his strength. Where he feels uncertain, be his confidence. Where he feels tired, be his renewal. Remind him who he is in You. I lift up our children before You. I speak life into their identity, hope into their future, and truth into their hearts. May they grow in wisdom, stature, and favor with You and with man. Guard them from deception. Strengthen them in their faith. Let them walk boldly in the purpose You have ordained for them. Help me to be a safe place for my family. A helper, encourager, and intercessor. May our home be filled with Your presence, and may our marriage and household reflect Your glory. In Jesus' name, Amen.

Journal Reflection

What has God revealed to you in the secret place?

What area of your prayer life is He calling you to grow in?

What new strategy or instruction has He given you?

Write it down. Pray into it. Act on it.

SIX

CHAIN OF COMMAND HONORING GOD'S ORDER

God is Not the Author of Confusion

In the military, a chain of command is a structured line of authority. It keeps chaos off the battlefield and ensures that every soldier knows their role and responsibility. Without it, even the strongest army will collapse under disunity. Marriage is no different. God designed a divine chain of command not to oppress but to protect, empower, and unify. When we reject that order, we invite confusion. When we honor it, we gain protection and peace.

Understanding Submission Within God's Order

When we talk about the chain of command in marriage, the conversation often turns quickly to the word submission. For many, that word stirs up discomfort, resistance, or even pain. And yet, it is a word found not only in Scripture but in the very structure of Heaven's order. But here's the truth: Submission is one part of a greater strategy. It's not about control. It's about flow. It's about how God's design channels peace, protection, and purpose through the home.

In the Kingdom, submission is not a punishment; it's a posture. And when it's rightly understood, it becomes one of the most powerful expressions of faith, trust, and spiritual strength.

Before we can truly embrace it, we must untangle the lies surrounding it.

What Submission isn't:
- Submission is not silence.
- It's not agreeing with everything.
- It's not tolerating abuse.
- It's not becoming invisible.

God never asked a woman to give up her voice or her value. He asked her to trust His order, a divine structure where love and leadership flow together under His covering.

Submission is:
- Spiritual alignment
- Willing cooperation under God's leadership
- Obedience to Christ, willingly embraced, not a status forced upon you

Submission is power under control. It's the decision to yield; not out of weakness, but from deep trust in the God who sees all and leads well. As Scripture says, "Wives, submit to your husbands, as is fitting in the Lord" (Colossians 3:18, ESV). Submission is first unto Christ, and from that place it flows into marriage. It is not blind surrender to a man's will, but a faith-filled posture that trusts God's order and believes His leadership unlocks protection, blessing, and peace.

Why Order Matters in Marriage

A household without spiritual order becomes a battleground of competing wills. But when we honor God's design, peace flows because everyone understands their role and responsibility. God's model is not a hierarchy of value; it's a hierarchy of function. In God's divine chain of command:

1. God is the head of Christ
2. Christ is the head of man
3. Man is the head of the wife
4. The wife is a co-laborer in the mission
   (See 1 Corinthians 11:3)

This structure was never meant to control. It's not about dominance; it's about divine accountability. Even within the Godhead, there is order. The Father, the Son, and the Holy Spirit are one. Equal in essence, yet distinct in role. Jesus submits to the Father. The Spirit proceeds from the Son. There is no competition, only cooperation. If perfect unity exists in divine order, how much more do we need it in marriage? A husband leads as Christ leads with sacrifice, service, and love. A wife responds not with resistance but with strength wrapped in honor. Order doesn't make you lesser. It positions you to receive.

What if He's Not Submitted to Christ?

This is one of the most tender and honest questions a wife can ask: "How do I submit to someone who isn't submitted to God?" The answer isn't compromising silence; it's Spirit-led wisdom. You are not called to follow sin. You are not required to silence your voice. But you are called to walk in a way that reflects alignment. When your husband's leadership falters, your posture still matters. Because the way you respond can either reflect the fear of man or trust in God. Here's what God calls you to:

- Stay aligned with truth even if he's off course
- Speak truth in love, not in pride

- Maintain a posture of honor without enabling dysfunction
- Set boundaries when needed without stepping out of divine order
- Let your conduct preach louder than your correction

"Likewise, wives, be subject to your own husbands, so that even if some do not obey the word, they may be won without a word by the conduct of their wives" (1 Peter 3:1, ESV).

Submission is Your Safety

There's a message that has deeply resonated with wives around the world, a teaching from Prophetess Maggie Elias that paints a powerful picture of submission using the imagery of an umbrella in the rain. She teaches that:

> *The man, no matter how little you view him, is made to handle the rain. You weren't made to bear it but to hold up what you can. If God gave you a man that feels heavy, then He made you strong enough to carry him—in prayer, in patience, and in honor.*

I love this analogy. This doesn't mean a wife has no voice. It doesn't mean she's called to tolerate sin or abuse. It means that submission is not about the condition of the man, it's about the assignment of the wife.

> *"If my man is not doing what he was made to do, it's because I, as his wife, am not holding him up."*

This is such a weighty charge, but it's also freeing. Because it reminds us that submission is not reactive; it's proactive obedience.

"If you think submission is because the man is doing what you believe is right, you've missed your assignment before God."

That line cut deeply. God will not measure our obedience by our husband's performance. He will measure it by how we respond to His voice. We don't submit because our husbands are perfect. We submit because our God is perfect. And when we align with His order, even when it's hard, we unlock His protection, His power, and His peace.

Excerpt from a teaching by Prophetess Maggie Elias, 2024 (Instagram Reel)

Military Parallel: Rank is About Mission, Not Worth

In the military, a general and a private may hold different ranks, but they are equally essential. The difference in rank isn't about worth, it's about responsibility. It's about who carries what and how the mission moves forward. The same is true in marriage. When we embrace God's divine order, we align with a strategy that wins. When we reject it, we often find ourselves fighting the wrong battles, or worse, fighting the one we're supposed to be covering. Submission is not about who's stronger. It's about who's submitted. And in the Kingdom, submission is a strategic strength, not a relational weakness.

Submission is like being meek. Jesus said, "Blessed are the meek, for they shall inherit the earth" (Matthew 5:5, ESV). Meekness is not weakness; it's disciplined power under divine command. It's knowing you could take control but choosing instead to trust God's authority and timing. In marriage, the wife who understands meekness and submission walks like a quiet general in the Spirit. She doesn't need to prove her strength. She postures herself in honor, and Heaven responds.

Submission & Humility — The Example of Christ

Many wives wrestle with submission because the world has twisted it into a symbol of oppression. But in the Kingdom, submission is the posture of Jesus. "Let this mind be in you which was also in Christ Jesus" (Philippians 2:5, ESV). Jesus is fully God, equal in glory, majesty, and power. Yet when He came to earth, He chose submission. He didn't demand His rights. He didn't resist the Father's will. He humbled Himself because He understood the assignment. "Though he was in the form of God, he did not count equality with God a thing to be grasped but emptied himself... and humbled himself by becoming obedient to the point of death" (Philippians 2:6–8, ESV). Jesus submitted not out of inferiority but intention. He knew that the mission required humility; and so does yours... Your mission also requires humility.

Posture Precedes Power

What God showed me in prayer is this: if I posture myself, Heaven will posture my husband. Even when the request is small, like avoid using canned food because he doesn't like preservatives. I've learned that submission doesn't require agreement with the resolution in order to walk in obedience. Sometimes, the very things I think are "not a big deal" are the exact places God is testing the posture of my heart.

For context, my husband is very health conscious. He pays attention to how he feeds our family because he believes that caring for our bodies is a part of loving us well. He believes God holds him accountable for how he protects us, not just spiritually, but physically too. So, when he says he doesn't want us eating canned foods, it's not about control. It's about conviction. It's his way of stewarding the family God gave him. But I didn't always see it that way. We grew up eating canned food. It wasn't seen as harmful; it was just normal. And when my husband would make these kinds of requests, part of me resisted, not because I wanted to rebel, but because I didn't see the problem. But in prayer, the Holy Spirit gently corrected me: "He's not asking you to sin. He's not asking you to disobey My Word. He's trying to love his family in the best ways he knows how, and I want you to honor that." That moment was a turning point. I realized that submission isn't always about agreeing with the situation at hand, but about trusting God's order that governs it. It's not about whether I see the reasoning clearly. It's about whether I believe that God is working through the structure He designed.

Now, when my husband says something that I wouldn't have chosen myself, I try to pause and ask, "Is this about preference... or posture?" It's not always as easy as it sounds. Sometimes, it takes a moment to get my flesh out of the way, but the Holy Spirit is faithful in convicting my heart. Because when I posture myself under God's order, I'm not just following a man. I'm obeying a mandate. And here's what I saw so clearly: If my husband's request is off, God will reveal that to him. As I bow in obedience, I can prophetically declare that my husband is bowing too. As I lift my hands in surrender, I can declare that my husband lifts his hands to God. We are one flesh. And my alignment invites Heaven's intervention. If Moses could lift his hands and shift the outcome of a battle (Exodus 17), then I can lift my hands in surrender and watch God move in my home.

You are a submissive wife. You're not surrendering to a man's opinion. You're surrendering to God's order, trusting that He can speak, correct, and shape both of you as you walk in obedience. And that... is where power flows.

For the Wife Who's Struggling to Submit

If you're struggling to submit. You're not weak. You're not rebellious. You're not a failure as a wife. You're human. You're

74

growing. Submission in a broken world, with imperfect people, can feel risky. But in the Kingdom, submission is not about perfection; it's about posture. It's about choosing trust when your flesh wants control. Jesus didn't submit because it was easy. He submitted because He saw the bigger picture. He knew the outcome. He was yielding to His design. And when you submit, not blindly, but in faith, you're stepping into His example.

You are not weak; your strength is restrained by trust. You're not giving up your voice. You're yielding it to God. You're not laying down your power. You're learning how to wield it in the spirit. And just like Jesus, your obedience won't go unnoticed. God sees the private places where you bow. And He will reward what no one else understands. You're not bowing to man. You're bowing to God's plan. And that is where inheritance is released.

As you bow in surrender, you will rise in strength. The next chapter will prepare you for what your obedience will require. The Armor of God.

Prayer

Father, I humble myself before You. Not because I feel small but because I trust You with what's beyond my control. Teach me the strength of meekness and submission. The kind of quiet trust that breaks walls and shifts atmospheres. Where I have resisted Your order, forgive me. Where fear has made me strive instead of submitting, heal me. I don't want to fight for power. I want to walk in purpose. Even when I don't understand my husband's reasoning, help me trust that You are still working. Help me honor the structure You set so that my home can flow in peace. I bow before You, believing that as I do, You are lifting my husband and leading our family. I receive the inheritance of the meek. I receive the peace of obedience, and I trust you to be my reward. In Jesus' name, Amen.

Journal Reflection

Where have I confused meekness with weakness in my role as a wife?

Have I been resisting my husband's leadership in small, subtle ways?

How would my perspective change if I viewed submission as a prophetic partnership with God rather than a loss of control?

Is there a specific area where God is asking me to trust Him more deeply?

SEVEN

THE ARMOR OF A WARRIOR BRIDE

A Wife at War Must be Covered

Every soldier, before stepping onto the battlefield, must be fully equipped, mentally focused, physically ready, and appropriately dressed. No one would dare enter a war zone wearing pajamas or sandals. Soldiers put on gear that protects, strengthens, and prepares them for the mission ahead. In marriage, a wife is not fighting her husband, she's fighting for the covenant. And that requires armor. This is the posture of a woman who is not just married but armored in submission. She is tender in love but trained in truth. She is not silent; she is positioned. Covered by Christ and equipped with His Word, she does not crumble under pressure, she stands.

In this chapter, we discover how each piece of spiritual armor equips you to win the battles that matter without losing your identity, your dignity, or your faith.

THE BELT OF TRUTH

"Stand therefore, having fastened on the belt of truth, and having put on the breastplate of righteousness…" (Ephesians 6:14, ESV).

From Fig Leaves to Full Covering

When Adam and Eve sinned, their eyes were opened, but not in the way that brought revelation. Their spiritual sight dimmed, and their natural sight took over. They became aware of their nakedness. Not because God's glory had disappeared but because sin distorted their ability to perceive it. Once they were clothed in God's presence, now they were distracted by shame. They could no longer see God or themselves rightly.

In their desperation, they reached for what was close and familiar: fig leaves. Genesis 3:7 (NKJV) says they "sewed fig leaves together and made themselves coverings." The word used for 'coverings' in some translations can be rendered as a belt or loincloth. This was an attempt to secure themselves. But it was fragile. Temporary. Insufficient. That's what happens when we try to cover ourselves apart from God. As wives, when we feel vulnerable or ashamed in marriage, we reach for modern-day fig leaves:

- Silence because speaking up feels risky.
- Busyness, to avoid dealing with what hurts.
- Control because surrender feels too vulnerable.
- Pretending to be okay when we're not.

But God, in His mercy, doesn't leave us in our fig leaves. He offers something stronger: the Belt of Truth. This belt is not decorative, it's foundational. It holds everything else in place. And it's not just truth about facts, it's truth about identity, purpose, and perspective. Jesus said, "If you abide in my word, you are truly my disciples, and you will know the truth, and the truth will set you free." (John 8:31–32, ESV). The truth sets your heart, your home, and your mind free from deception. When we wrap ourselves in the truth of God's Word:

- We stop covering ourselves with coping mechanisms
- We stop living by emotions
- We start standing in who God says we are

When your heart is clean and uncluttered by shame or falsehood, you will see God, not just in eternity, but in your husband, your home, and your covenant. Truth restores your vision. It's time to drop the fig leaves, fasten the belt, and let truth hold you together where shame once tore you apart.

THE BREASTPLATE OF RIGHTEOUSNESS

"...and having put on the breastplate of righteousness..." (Ephesians 6:14, ESV)

Protected by His Perfection

This protects the heart, the most vital and vulnerable place in marriage. In battle, a soldier's heart is always a prime target. In marriage, your heart is also under constant attack. The enemy knows that if he can corrupt your motives, distort your identity, or infect your intentions, he can damage the flow of love, trust, and unity in your home. That's why God doesn't ask us to protect our hearts with our own goodness. He covers us with His righteousness.

The breastplate we wear is not handcrafted by our own effort. It's not made of perfection in communication, flawless submission, or daily acts of kindness. If that were the case, none of us would be protected. Our righteousness on our best day is like filthy rags before a Holy God (Isaiah 64:6). But in Jesus, we are made new. He is our righteousness (1 Corinthians 1:30), and it is His obedience, His purity, and His sacrifice that shield our hearts. Just as we needed Jesus to save us, we need Him just as desperately to sustain us, especially in marriage. We don't graduate from grace once we say, 'I do', in fact, we lean on it more deeply. Every time we are tempted to respond in pride, bitterness, self-pity, or control, the enemy wants us to fight with flesh and self-righteousness. But the breastplate reminds us: our defense is not our behavior, it's our dependence on Christ.

God honors a heart that thirst after righteousness. Not perfection but pursuit. He satisfies the wife who is craving alignment, not the one striving to be flawless. Marriage will expose your weaknesses. It will highlight your need for humility, forgiveness, patience, and deep healing. But this isn't to shame you; it's to anchor you. You were never meant to carry the weight of being 'enough' on your own. You were meant to abide. Your spiritual armor isn't held up by willpower; it's fastened by surrender. The moment you try to love your husband in your own strength, you will burn out. The moment you attempt to build a godly home on your own efforts, you will feel defeated. But when you remember that Christ has already overcome, and you are hidden in Him (Colossians 3:3), you will find rest, even in war. So, wear the breastplate boldly. Not because you've done everything right but because Jesus did. And in Him, you are secured.

THE SHOES OF PEACE

"...and, as shoes for your feet, having put on the readiness given by the gospel of peace." (Ephesians 6:15, ESV)

Abigail: A Wife Who Walked in Peace

Peace isn't the absence of conflict, it's the presence of God in the middle of it. The 'shoes of the gospel of peace' symbolize readiness, stability, and a spirit grounded in the peace of God. Peace that not only calms our own soul but brings peace into hostile environments. That is precisely what Abigail did in 1 Samuel 25. Abigail was married to Nabal, a harsh and foolish man whose name literally means *'fool'*. He was disrespectful, arrogant, and reckless. When David sent men to humbly request supplies after protecting Nabal's men in the wilderness, Nabal insulted them, triggering David's wrath.

Abigail didn't live in peace, but she walked in peace. She didn't let her husband's dysfunction define her demeanor. She remained discerning, wise, and grounded, even while married to someone who sowed discord. When Abigail heard what Nabal had done, she prepared an offering, gathered supplies, and rode out to meet David herself. This was a dangerous move. David was coming with 400 armed men, ready to destroy every male in Nabal's household. But Abigail didn't show up with panic. She showed up with presence. She knelt before David, honored him, and appealed to his future. She reminded him of who he was in God and how avenging himself with blood would stain his calling. "When the Lord has fulfilled for my lord every good thing, he promised... my lord will not have on his conscience the staggering burden of needless bloodshed..." 1 Samuel 25:30–31 (paraphrased).

Abigail didn't just bring words of peace. She carried the weight of peace. Her humility, wisdom, and courage diffused a volatile situation. She brought peace where a sword was already drawn. David's entire course of action shifted after encountering Abigail. He said: "Blessed be the Lord, the God of Israel, who sent you this day to meet me! Blessed be your discretion, and blessed be you, who have kept me this day from bloodguilt and from working salvation with my own hand!" (1 Samuel 25:32–33, ESV). Abigail saved lives because she was a peacemaker, not a peacekeeper. She didn't avoid conflict, she confronted it with a calm spirit, wise words, and a peaceful posture.

The shoes of peace don't mean we avoid confrontation or pretend everything is okay. They mean we walk into difficult places carrying the atmosphere of Heaven. We become bridges instead of barriers. We speak to the future, not just the problem. Abigail modeled that. And for wives today, she is proof that peace protects life.

THE SHIELD OF FAITH

"Take up the shield of faith, with which you can extinguish all the flaming darts of the evil one." (Ephesians 6:16, ESV)

Leah and the Shield of Faith — Choosing Praise Over Pain

The Shield of Faith is given to us to extinguish the flaming arrows of the enemy; those arrows that come in the form of rejection, insecurity, disappointment, and comparison. Leah, the wife of Jacob, knew those arrows well. She was not the wife Jacob chose. She was given to him through deceit and lived in the shadow of her sister, Rachel, the one Jacob truly loved. Leah longed to be seen. To be wanted. To be chosen. So, she did what many wives do when they feel unseen, she tried to earn love through performance. With every child she birthed, she hoped her husband would finally notice her.

- "Surely my husband will love me now." (Genesis 29:32, NKJV)

- "Because the Lord has heard that I am unloved, He has therefore given me this son also." (Genesis 29:33, NKJV)

- "Now this time my husband will become attached to me, because I have borne him three sons." (Genesis 29:34, NKJV)

Each son's name reflected her deep ache. She wrapped her identity around Jacob's attention, and each time he withheld it, her heart took another hit. But then came Judah.

- "This time I will praise the Lord." (Genesis 29:35, NKJV)

This was Leah's turning point. She stopped chasing Jacob's validation and started anchoring her heart in God's faithfulness. Her focus shifted from pain to praise. That moment, when she chose worship over her worthiness is when her shield went up. Faith doesn't always remove the pain. But it positions us to respond differently. Leah was still unloved by Jacob, but she was now anchored by a deeper truth: God saw her, heard her, and was writing her story.

Through Judah, the son she birthed in praise, came the royal line of David. And generations later, Jesus Christ would be born through the same tribe. The woman who was overlooked by man became the vessel for the Messiah. Leah teaches us that faith is not about pretending things are perfect. It's about choosing to believe God is present and worthy even when things feel painful. It's saying, 'This time, I will praise the Lord', even when the situation hasn't changed.

When the arrows of rejection or comparison come flying, lift your shield. Don't reach for performance, reach for praise. Don't let your identity be shaped by who sees you. Let it be shaped by the One who formed you. Faith says: I may not be chosen by man, but I am seen, loved, and already chosen by God.

THE HELMET OF SALVATION

"Take the helmet of salvation…" — (Ephesians 6:17, ESV)

Mary and the Helmet of Salvation — A Mind Aligned with Purpose

The Helmet of Salvation protects our mind. It secures our identity and guards our thoughts when fear, shame, or uncertainty try to take over. It's more than an assurance of eternal life. It's the covering that keeps us grounded in God's truth about who we are and what He has called us to. Mary, the mother of Jesus, is a powerful example of a woman who wore the Helmet of Salvation well. When the angel Gabriel appeared to her and told her that she would conceive the Son of God, she had every reason to be overwhelmed. She was young. She was not yet married. Her future was uncertain. And yet her response was full of peace and surrender.

"Behold, I am the servant of the Lord; let it be to me according to your word." (Luke 1:38, ESV). Mary didn't let fear rule her thoughts. She didn't argue with her assignment. She didn't spiral into anxiety. She guarded her mind with truth. She received the Word of God, and she submitted to it, even when it would cost her comfort and reputation. She could have worried about what people would think. She could have focused on Joseph's reaction. She could have let the weight of carrying something so holy drive her to panic. But instead, she anchored her identity in God's Word. That is the Helmet of Salvation in action.

She carried Jesus, not just in her womb, but in her mind. She let the truth of what God was doing overshadow the opinions of others. She meditated on His promises. She hid His words in her heart. She believed what He said. And as she walked out her purpose, she stayed mentally rooted in what God declared. She stood at the cross. She remained with the disciples. She didn't just give birth to salvation, she lived under its covering.

Mary teaches us that the Helmet of Salvation is not just about what we believe about God. It's also about what we believe about ourselves when God speaks. Will we agree with His calling? Will we align our thoughts with His Word? Will we protect our minds from the lies that tell us we're not enough?

Your mind is a battlefield. But salvation is your covering. Put on the Helmet. Let God's truth be louder than fear. Let His Word shape how you think, how you see yourself, and how you walk in your calling. Mary did. And through her surrendered mind, the Savior came forth.

THE SWORD OF THE SPIRIT

"Take the helmet of salvation, and the sword of the Spirit, which is the word of God." (Ephesians 6:17, ESV)

The Sword of the Spirit is not just information, it is revelation. The word used in this verse for 'word' is not *Logos*, which refers to the written Word, it's *Rhema*. *Rhema* is the living, specific, Spirit-breathed word of God that speaks directly into your moment. It can be:

- A verse of Scripture the Holy Spirit highlights with power and urgency
- A prophetic word delivered through someone else
- A still, small voice telling you what to do, when to move, what to say, or when to be silent

Where *Logos* fills your heart, *Rhema* cuts through the atmosphere.

Rhema Looks Like This:
- You're praying over your marriage, and suddenly, one verse comes alive in your spirit, that's *Rhema*.
- You're confused about what to do, and the Holy Spirit tells you clearly: "Leave. This is not My will." That's *Rhema*.
- You're in a difficult marriage and people are pressuring you to stay, but God speaks and says, "I did not join this. I'm calling you out." That's *Rhema*.

Rhema is not always comfortable. It may be unconventional, countercultural, or completely different from what others expect. But it will always align with the heart and holiness of God.

"My sheep hear my voice, and I know them, and they follow me." (John 10:27, ESV).

Sometimes, Rhema will come to rescue you:
- From a counterfeit marriage
- From something deadly parading as love
- From years of abuse and spiritual confusion

Other times, it will come to refine you:
- "Stay, and I'll show you how to stand."
- "Forgive, and I'll fight for you."
- "Speak truth, even if it costs comfort."

Rhema doesn't always make sense to people, but it brings clarity to the spirit. And when God gives it, you are not only released to follow it, but you are also equipped.

You have a sword. You don't need to stay bound in confusion. You don't need to fight in your flesh. Ask God for His Word, and when He gives it, declare it. Obey it. Trust it.

A Word to the Engaged and Courting

If you're not yet married. If you are engaged or currently courting, you still need to be armored. This is the time to seek God, not just about the wedding, but about the marriage. Take the time to go before God and ask Him: "What are You saying about this relationship?" "Is this the person I am meant to partner with?" Don't move forward on emotions alone. Don't assume love is enough. God will give you clear instructions to prepare you or to protect you. He is a good Father. He reveals red flags before they become regrets. He gives wisdom when we ask. "If any of you lacks wisdom, let him ask God, who gives generously to all without reproach, and it will be given him." (James 1:5, ESV).

Ask God for confirmation. Listen carefully. Don't just armor up for a future you haven't discerned. Let God be the architect of your covenant before you build it.

In the next chapter, we'll look at another weapon, your tongue. Armor up as we tackle tactical communication.

Prayer

Father, I come to You today acknowledging that I cannot win these battles alone. Thank You for providing spiritual armor that protects, empowers, and aligns me with Your will. Clothe me in truth. Guard my heart with righteousness. Let my feet walk in peace. Strengthen me with faith. Thank You for covering my mind. Let Your Word be the sword that I carry boldly. Remove every impurity that clouds my vision. Align my heart with Your truth so I can discern rightly, walk humbly, and stand boldly. Show me what You're saying about my marriage. Remove every voice of confusion and highlight what is real, and righteous. I surrender my assumptions, my plans, and my fears. I yield to Your strategy. Armor me not just for battle, but for victory. In Jesus' name, Amen.

Journal Reflection

What piece of the armor have I neglected in this season?

Am I fighting in my flesh or with the Word of God?

What specific Rhema (spoken) word has God given me for this marriage or relationship?

Have I asked God for clarity about the person I am courting or planning to marry?

What scriptures can I begin to speak daily over my marriage?

EIGHT

TACTICAL
COMMUNICATION

Words as Weapons or Healing Tools

In battle, poor communication can cost lives. In marriage, it can cost connection, trust, and peace. You can be right in content, but completely wrong in tone, timing, or delivery. That's why communication must be tactical: intentional, Spirit-led, and aligned with your mission. As a wife, your words have power. Power to build up or tear down, to invite healing or deepen wounds. This chapter is about learning how to speak with purpose, not just emotion. To use your voice without using it to destroy.

Jesus said, "Blessed are the peacemakers…" Not those who simply avoid conflict, but those who take bold, Spirit-led steps to create redemptive peace. They know when to speak, when to wait, and when to war in prayer. You are not just a responder. The way you communicate can usher in the presence of God, or release confusion and chaos.

Communication is Prophetic

Communication should be prophetic. Every time you speak, you are agreeing with a spirit. Either the Spirit of God, or something else. Your words can either align with Heaven or echo the voice of the real enemy. The enemy's strategy has always been rooted in language. In the Garden of Eden, Satan didn't swing a sword; he planted a suggestion. He used twisted communication to corrupt trust, distort identity, and destroy unity. He still does that today, especially in marriages. Jesus said, "The words that I have spoken to you are spirit and life" (John 6:63, ESV). When a wife speaks, she's not just expressing herself. She's either prophesying life into the atmosphere of her home or giving voice to the lies that aim to tear it down.

Ask yourself: When I speak, whose voice am I echoing? Do my words rehearse the report of God, or the enemy's accusations? This is the gravity of your role: Your tongue can be anointed, or weaponized. That's why the enemy loves to provoke irritation, offense, and defensiveness. He knows if he can get control of your mouth, he can influence your marriage. But the good news is this: when your communication is yielded to the Holy Spirit, your words become instruments of warfare, words that disarm, protect, and establish God's peace.

If you want to see transformation in your husband, your home, and even your own soul, you must become a woman who speaks life even when it's hard. This isn't about flattery or pretending everything's okay. Speaking life means choosing to align your words with Heaven's report, even when your emotions are trying to declare something else. I know we often say that words are powerful, but one of the greatest lessons I've ever learned is that only one Word carries great power, and that is the Word of the Lord. Our words hold weight only when they echo what God has already spoken. You are never more powerful than when your words are His.

Speak Like You're Speaking to God: Reverence in Communication

Communication is always better in a humble tone. Think about how you speak when you're in prayer. You come before God with honesty, yes, but also with humility. Even when you're confused, disappointed, or deeply burdened, you still speak with reverence because you're mindful of who you're talking to. That same principle can transform how you speak to your husband. Not because you're worshiping him, but because you honor the position God gave him. Scripture says, "Submit to one another out of reverence for Christ. Wives, submit yourselves to your own husbands as you do to the Lord." (Ephesians 5:21–22, NIV) That reverence is not limited to worship services and quiet time. It should influence how we approach every conversation. Not just the calm ones, but the conflicted ones too. When we shift our posture, we shift the atmosphere.

There was a time in my own marriage when my husband and I were in the middle of a heated conversation. He was telling me what I wasn't doing right, and I felt like he was being unfair. I stood there quietly, but inside I was bubbling. I couldn't wait for him to finish so I could explain why he was wrong, and how much he was overlooking. But something unexpected happened. The moment he finished speaking, and I opened my mouth to respond, what came out wasn't sharp or defensive. It wasn't even rehearsed. The Holy Spirit interrupted my flesh and said through me, "I understand. And I'm sorry. I'm going to do better." Even my husband looked surprised. And so was I. Because we both knew what I was about to say. But God stepped in. He snatched the words that could have cut and replaced them with words that healed. And just like that, the tension gave way to tenderness. It was a holy moment because it was a God moment. That's what happens when you speak from a place of reverence. Your tone softens. Your posture humbles. And you begin to see your husband not just as your man, but as God's son; beloved, flawed, and entrusted to your care.

Now, let me be clear. I don't always get it right. And you won't either. There are days I say things I regret. Moments, I choose pride instead of peace. But the beauty of grace is this: God never expected perfection. He expects surrender. It's not your mistake that disqualifies you; it's your decision to stay in it. Allow the Holy Spirit to grow you from your errors.

Jesus said, "Love one another as I have loved you" (John 13:34, ESV). That kind of love doesn't show up only in gentle moments. It's tested in tension. It's revealed in the tone of your voice and the posture of your heart. So, speak like you're talking to God. Not because your husband is God, but because God is in him, and He is in the conversation.

The Battlefield of the Tongue

"The tongue has the power of life and death, and those who love it will eat its fruit" (Proverbs 18:21, NIV). Every marriage faces moments of tension. But what makes or breaks those moments isn't what you feel, it's how you release it. Unfiltered communication is like firing without aiming. It's loud, messy, and often causes collateral damage. Tactical communication, on the other hand, is like precision targeting. You speak truth, but with timing, care, and clear intention. And when your heart is submitted to the Holy Spirit, even correction can sound like love. Below are some tactical tools that I've learned over the years.

TACTICAL TOOLS FOR REAL CONVERSATIONS

Use 'I' Statements, not 'You' Accusations
    X "You never listen to me."

✓ "I feel unheard when I try to share something."

Why it works: It invites openness instead of defensiveness. It keeps the conversation about your experience, not your spouse's flaws.

Practice Emotional Intelligence. Pause and reflect before speaking
- What am I really feeling?
- What do I need right now?
- Is this the right moment to talk about this?

Wisdom tip: Never launch a hard conversation when either of you are hungry, tired, or emotionally flooded.

Don't Fight to Win, Fight to Understand
- Marriage is not a courtroom. You're not trying to 'win' a case. You're trying to preserve a covenant.

Tactical wives don't attack. They don't ignore truth, but they wrap it in humility and honor. Your goal is never to overpower, but to restore unity.

Listen to Understand, Not Just to Respond
- Try saying: "So what I hear you saying is…" or "It sounds like this made you feel…"

When your husband feels understood, he's more likely to open up. Safety in communication comes from feeling seen, not corrected.

Watch Tone, Timing, and Touch
- Tone: Are you firm but loving, or sharp and sarcastic?

- Timing: Are you choosing a moment when connection is possible?
- Touch: A gentle touch on the shoulder, sitting close, or holding hands softens even the hardest conversations.

When Silence is the Strategy
- Silence becomes a strategy when it's led by God, not by offense. There's a difference between silence that avoids and silence that protects peace.

Daily Reconnection Routine: Ask, Repent, Repeat:

When I used to facilitate a marriage small group at my church, I came across this strategy that deeply impacted me. I don't remember the original source, but it helped to shaped how I understood reconciliation in marriage.

Here's the practice: At the end of each day, before you go to bed, ask your spouse two questions:

1. "What did I do today that made you feel loved?" Then do more of it.

2. "What did I do today that hurt you or felt off?" Then repent. Acknowledge it. And try not to do it again.

It reminded me of how sin separates us from God. Not because He leaves us, but because we pull back. Marriage can feel the same. We can be in the same house, same bed, and feel miles apart. This kind of nightly check-in brings us back to oneness. It's not about being perfect. It's about being present, honest, and tenderhearted toward one another. Just like we seek daily repentance with God, we should seek daily reconnection with our spouse.

When You're Misunderstood

There will be times when you do everything right and still feel unheard. There will be moments when you express yourself the best way you know how, and your husband still doesn't understand your heart. One of the most powerful biblical examples of this is Hannah. Hannah's story reminds us that even though our husbands love us deeply, they may not always understand the burdens we carry. Elkanah looked at Hannah's tears and could not comprehend the depth of her longing for a child. He asked her, "Am I not more to you than ten sons?" (1 Samuel 1:8, ESV). His love was real, but it could not satisfy the cry that only God could answer. There will be times when our husbands cannot interpret the grief, the longing, or the weight on our hearts, but like Hannah, we must learn to pour out our soul before the Lord, even when our husbands misread us.

Another moment with Hanna is when she was praying with such deep anguish that her words weren't even audible. Eli, the priest, saw her lips moving and misjudged her completely. But Hannah didn't lash out. She clarified with grace and stood her ground with dignity. And ultimately, God responded, not just to her words, but to the posture of her heart. Sometimes your husband and others may misinterpret your intention. But even then, you are seen by God. He understands what your heart is really saying.

I've learned that trying to be heard in the heat of the moment doesn't always work. There are times when I am going back and forth with my husband, and I realize I'm not being heard. Either emotions are too high, or the timing just isn't right. So, I do something different now: I step away from the conversation, and

I let him have the last word. Not because I'm giving in, but because I've learned that peace is more powerful than proving a point. After I walk away, I take a moment to breathe, pray, and gather my thoughts. Then, I send him a text message. Not while I'm still heated. I've learned that lesson too. There have been so many times where I've typed out heated messages ready to press send, and the Holy Spirit stopped me mid-sentence. I can't tell you how many texts didn't make it out because the Holy Spirit caught them. And I'm so grateful. Because when you speak from your emotions instead of your spirit, you end up saying things that bruise rather than bless.

A few of those heated ones did slip through. And every time, the Holy Spirit convicted me. I had to apologize, repent, and deal with the damage my words caused. But I'm growing. I'm becoming more sensitive to the Holy Spirit. Now, more often than not, I pause. I sit with God. I let my heart settle before I try to express anything. And then, I process the message.

I take my time to type out what I need to say, not from a place of pride, but from a place of peace. I explain how I was feeling, what I meant, and why it mattered to me. I don't accuse. I don't attack. I just share carefully and prayerfully. And it works. Every time. There has never been a time when I've sent a message like that, and my husband didn't respond with love. He'll often say things like:

- "Baby, I'm sorry."
- "I understand."
- "Please forgive me."
- "I'm going to do better."

Those are the responses I want, not because I need to be right, but because I want peace. Peace is the win. So, if you ever feel like you're not being heard in the moment, pause instead of pushing. Let the Lord settle your heart. Don't send a message from your flesh. Send it from your spirit. Let your words be covered in wisdom. "Let your speech always be gracious, seasoned with salt, so that you may know how you ought to answer..." (Colossians 4:6, ESV). Let the Holy Spirit speak through you, even through your fingertips. Sometimes the most powerful conversation happens after the conversation ends.

When it's Not a Big Fight, But the Small Irritations

The real battle isn't always in the blowups, it's in the buildup. It's not the huge arguments that wear you down. It's the small, repetitive irritations. The daily disruptions. The unmet expectations quietly gather until they harden into resentment. But even in these small moments, the Holy Spirit offers us tactical training. He teaches us that how we handle the little things reveals the condition of our heart. One of the things I've learned is this: Whenever something feels difficult or inconvenient, it's often a divine invitation to grow. It's God offering me a moment of sacrifice on a silver platter. And if I'm honest, those moments don't always feel holy. They feel annoying. They really test me. But when I step back and ask, "Lord, what are You trying to teach me through this?" That's when growth begins.

When my husband and I first started living together, I noticed he had a habit of leaving bottles open: mouthwash, oil, you name it. I would accidentally hit a bottle and suddenly, the kitchen would be flooded with cooking oil or the bathroom flooded with mouthwash, causing a huge mess. At first, it really got under my skin. I wanted to say something every time. But the Holy Spirit started training me. Instead of complaining, I just started checking and closing them quietly. What I didn't realize at the time was that I was learning how to cover his weakness instead of exposing it.

And every time I closed a bottle cap, I was planting a seed, a seed of patience, grace, and love.

And let's talk about the toilet seat. You know what I'm talking about. That infamous frustration that seems to show up in every marriage at some point. It bothered me too. But again, I heard the Holy Spirit whisper: "Why not just check it before you sit?" It was so simple, but it shifted something in me. Rather than turning it into a pattern of offense, I began turning it into a habit of grace. Just like that, the toilet seat was no longer a battlefield. It became an altar. A place to die to self, again and again.

Here's the beautiful part: I started seeing change. Now my husband closes the bottles. He puts the toilet seat down almost always. Things that used to be daily annoyances are no longer concerns. Well… sometimes in the middle of the night, I still find myself closing the seat, but now it's usually because my son left it up, not my husband! Grace works. You really do reap what you sow. Maybe not instantly, but in time. The seeds I sowed in silence began to produce fruit within the everyday habits of my home.

But it didn't stop there. I started to notice the flip side too. I can be messy sometimes—especially when I'm rushing out the door and leave makeup scattered across the counter. My daughter, now ten, loves to play in my makeup as well. Yet my husband never complains. Instead, he quietly picks things up. He even washes our hair brushes and combs until they're squeaky clean. He covers us in our messes the way I learned to cover him in his. The truth is, my husband isn't a complaining man. If he ever does mention something, it's because it's truly gotten out of hand. Most of the time, he simply takes responsibility and does what needs to be done. When I look back, I realize God was teaching us both. I was reaping what I sowed in silence, but he was also reaping what he had sown all along, gentleness, steadiness, and patience. In our marriage, we don't just correct each other's weaknesses; we've learned to cover them. And in that covering, God has allowed love to grow.

Now hear me clearly: I'm not saying don't talk about these things. Have the conversation. Express how you feel. But don't nag about it. Don't complain every time. Don't let it become the soundtrack of your home. Maybe for you, it's not bottles or the toilet seat. Perhaps it's clothes left on the floor. Pick them up. Quietly. You're not just doing chores, you're helping him. And helping your husband might look like simply helping him get his clothes off the floor. Have conversations. Be honest. But don't weaponize your words. Say it with grace, and then let the Holy Spirit do the rest. Your part is obedience. God's part is transformation.

What Are You Sowing?

Every day, with every small response, you are building something. The only question is: What kind of house are you building? Are you sowing irritation, sarcasm, or passive-aggression? Or are you sowing patience, gentleness, and spiritual maturity? The fruit you see tomorrow is rooted in what you plant today. Ask the Holy Spirit:

- What am I being invited to overlook today for the sake of peace?
- Where can I cover instead of correct?
- What would it look like to serve without needing to be seen?

When you serve in these quiet ways, your husband may not always notice, but God does, and that is what truly matters. Do everything unto God. In due time, you will reap what you've sown. So, keep choosing love. Keep closing bottles. Keep checking the seat. Keep covering instead of always correcting. This is daily warfare. This is a sacred sacrifice. This is covenant communication.

Biblical Examples: Communication That Shaped Outcomes

✓ *Abigail and David – The Peace She Carried Was Strategic*

We've already talked about Abigail, Nabal's wife, when we explored the Shoes of Peace. But she's worth mentioning again here, because she didn't just walk in peace; she spoke with it. When David was on his way to destroy her household, Abigail met him with a heart full of discernment and words wrapped in humility. She spoke with purpose. Her communication was so powerful that it disarmed a man of war: "Please forgive the trespass of your servant. For the Lord will certainly make my lord a sure house, because my lord is fighting the battles of the Lord…" (1 Samuel 25:28, ESV) Abigail didn't just save lives; she spoke life. She redirected rage with honor and prophesied destiny instead of defending herself. True peacemakers are not silent; they are Spirit-led and strategically vocal. Words, when seasoned with wisdom, can change the course of conflict.

✗ *Moses Strikes the Rock – A Missed Moment of Reverence*

In Numbers 20:7–12, God told Moses to speak to the rock so water would flow. But Moses, worn out and angry, struck the rock instead, and misrepresented God to the people. "Listen, you rebels, shall we bring water for you out of this rock?" (Numbers 20:10, ESV) Water still came, but because of Moses' tone and disobedience, he lost something far more valuable: access to the Promised Land.

Even when the result looks successful, miscommunication can carry a cost. Tone, timing, obedience, and posture matter deeply, especially when we are called to represent God in the way we speak. To carry this further, effective communication also requires insight; truly knowing the one you are speaking to. In the next chapter, we will look at the field of intelligence: knowing your spouse.

Prayer

Father, thank You for showing me that my words matter. Thank You for the invitation to be a peacemaker. Not one who avoids truth, but one who carries Your heart into every conversation. Lord, forgive me for the moments I've spoken in pride or frustration. Forgive me for when I tried to be right instead of righteous. Wash my tongue. Heal the hearts I've hurt, including my own. Holy Spirit, make me more sensitive to Your leading. Quicken me before I speak from my flesh. Help me to acknowledge and receive your grace when I fail and help me rise in humility. Teach me how to speak with wisdom, reverence, and love. Let my tone carry truth, but always be seasoned with salt. Let my timing reflect patience. Let my silence be Spirit-led. And when I'm misunderstood, remind me that You see me. You know what I meant, and You hear what I couldn't say. Make me a woman who builds with her words. Make me a woman who speaks as one who has been with You. Make me a peacemaker. A daughter of God who reflects her Father in every conversation. In Jesus' name, Amen.

Journal Reflection

Heart Check-In: What patterns do I notice in the way I speak to my husband?

Is my tone rooted in peace or pride?

Do I speak to him with the same humility I use when I speak to God?

What's one time I spoke too quickly or too sharply? How can I repair that conversation, either with my words or with a grace-filled text?

What's one area of daily irritation (like the toilet seat, bottle caps, or laundry) where I'm being invited to cover instead of correct?

Promotion Checkpoint: Self-Evaluation

[ ] I invited the Holy Spirit into today's conversations
[ ] I spoke with grace even when I was frustrated
[ ] I chose peace over being right
[ ] I repented when I missed it
[ ] I remembered that God is present in every exchange
[ ] I spoke as a daughter of God called to build, not break

NINE

FIELD INTELLIGENCE KNOWING YOUR SPOUSE

Know the Field Before You Fight

In military strategy, before soldiers are deployed, intelligence is gathered about terrain, weather, the enemy's movements, and the location of resources. Why? Because you can't win in a territory you don't understand. Marriage is no different. You cannot fight for your husband if you do not understand how he thinks, feels, communicates, and process life. That's not control, it's wisdom. This chapter isn't about "fixing" your husband. It's about studying him with love, so that you can better serve, pray, and connect with the man God joined you to.

What Is Field Intelligence in Marriage?

Field intelligence means learning your husband's:

- Communication patterns
- Emotional triggers
- Love language
- Fears and dreams
- Patterns under stress
- Relationship with God

SIX INTELLIGENCE AREAS YOU SHOULD KNOW

1. His Respect Code

Before you can even begin learning your husband's love language, dreams, stress patterns, or communication style, you need to understand something deeper. His need for respect. The Bible makes it clear: "However, let each one of you love his wife as himself, and let the wife see that she respects her husband" (Ephesians 5:33, ESV). Respect is not flattery or silence. It's posture, tone, and honor. And for men, it is the most critical way they feel loved. I learned this the hard way.

Before my husband and I were married, he once took me to the San Souci Hotel to celebrate my birthday. As a tennis professional, he has coached the game at many hotels across Jamaica's north coast and has established connections with management in many of the hotels. I knew the dinner and entertainment were covered because of his relationship with them, and honestly, I didn't value it the way I should have. I felt like not much thought went into it because it didn't cost him financially. I didn't yet understand that the currency of relationship and the favor that flows from proximity is far more valuable than finances. My posture spoke louder than my words. In my mind, I wasn't being disrespectful, but my lack of joy and gratitude communicated that I didn't value him, or his gesture. And that night, my husband, still my boyfriend then, let me have it. He shared his heart in raw honesty: that I was selfish, ungrateful, and not seeing who he truly was or how he showed love. He wasn't just talking about that night. I have been like that! It hurt. I cried the entire night. But I thank God for that moment. Because that was the wake-up call that taught me I could lose a great man simply because I didn't know how to honor him.

I didn't know how to show appreciation. I believed I was entitled to more when I should have been cherishing what was already good. God has taught me so much since then. There have been times when my tone starts to shift in conversation with my husband, and I'll hear the Holy Spirit whisper: "Be careful how you're speaking to My son." It stops me every time. That's what we forget, our husbands are not just our partners. They are sons of God. And how we speak to them matters deeply to Him. When we correct with contempt or speak with sarcasm, we're not just damaging the relationship; we're disrespecting God's son. And the truth is, some of us are praying for our men to change when God is waiting for us to change the way we treat them. Respect unlocks the door to a man's heart. And when he feels respected, he responds with greater tenderness and care toward his wife. So, before we move into love languages or conflict styles, we must first ask:

- How does my husband interpret respect?
- What makes him feel dishonored?
- What makes him feel valued as a man?

Don't assume. Ask. Watch. Study. And above all, honor him as God's son, not just your spouse.

Dr. Emerson Eggerichs, author of *Love and Respect*, spent years counseling couples and discovered what he called "The Crazy Cycle": when a wife feels unloved, she reacts in ways that feel disrespectful to her husband. When a husband feels disrespected, he responds in ways that feel unloving to his wife. And around and around it goes. But when a wife chooses respect, even when she doesn't feel loved, and when a husband chooses love, even when he feels disrespected, it interrupts the cycle. It creates space for healing, not hostility. Dr Eggerichs didn't just write a book; he unveiled what the Bible already declared in Ephesians 5:33. His work confirms what God has said all along: women crave love, men need respect, and when both are honored, marriage thrives. As Dr. Eggerichs explains, a wife's call is to give her husband unconditional respect, just as a husband's call is to give his wife unconditional love.

Instead of waiting for your husband to perfectly demonstrate unconditional love before you respond with respect, focus on what God requires of you. Hold yourself accountable to offer respect regardless of his actions. This not only positions you to receive God's reward, but it also softens and opens your husband's heart, creating the space for him to love you more freely and unconditionally.

2. Know His Love Language
How does your husband best receive love?

- Words of Affirmation
- Acts of Service
- Physical Touch
- Quality Time
- Gifts

As a wife, your assignment includes your husband's heart. To serve him with wisdom, you must first study him with intention. Yes, this is spiritual. Yes, this is warfare. And yes, this is love. Just as we learn what pleases God, we must also know what ministers to our husbands. Even God has a love language, not one discovered through a personality quiz, but one revealed in scriptures and through intimacy and obedience. Throughout Scripture, God tells us what moves His heart and what He desires most, but sometimes, like wives in our own homes, we give God what we think He wants, rather than what He's actually asked for.

"Is this the kind of fast I have chosen...?" (Isaiah 58:5, NIV). "To loose the chains of injustice...to set the oppressed free..." (Isaiah 58:6, NIV). God told His people, "You're doing what looks spiritual, but it's not what I want." It's the same in marriage. You might be doing things you think your husband appreciates, but if you've never truly asked or observed, you could be missing the mark.

The late great Kenneth Hagin once shared a testimony that deeply shaped how I see obedience. He said that he had been pastoring a church for twelve years when the Lord Jesus visited him. Jesus said to him, "It's time for you to step into the first phase of your ministry." Kenneth Hagin was stunned. He responded, "My first phase? I've been ministering all this time, pastoring for twelve years." And Jesus answered, "Yes, but I never told you to do that." That moment redefined obedience for him, and it can do the same for us as wives. Are you doing what your husband need, or just what you assumed would work?

This past summer, the Lord gave me a fresh lesson on what it really means to be a helper in my marriage. My husband runs tennis camps whenever school breaks. For the previous camps, I would sometimes step in to help during lunchtime, serving the kids, waiting with those who were going home early, or covering small gaps when my husband was pulled into private lessons. But if I'm honest, I didn't approach it with the right heart. I was reluctant, because while I love being present with my children, I also looked forward to those camp hours as time for me to focus on my own projects. The Holy Spirit checked me: If you are his helper, you are his helper wherever the need shows up. That conviction stayed with me, and when this summer's camp came around, I shifted my posture. Instead of resisting, I prepared myself mentally and spiritually. Each morning, I knew that between 11:30 and 1:30, my assignment was to support my husband. That meant picking up lunch for the kids, serving them directly, and waiting for parents to pick up the half-day kids if my husband was tied up with lessons. I didn't wait for him to ask; I called to check in, anticipated his needs, and positioned myself to fill the gap.

The difference it made in his spirit was undeniable. He started sending me the sweetest messages in the middle of the day: "Thank you." "You're one in a million." "You're one of one." Those words came because my sacrificial help moved his heart. I lifted the weight off his shoulders. My help gave him rest, not just relief.

What I didn't expect was the increase that came through my willingness. One afternoon, while I was serving lunch, a parent walked in asking about lessons. There was no other staff available, and my husband was on court with a client. Because I was there, I was able to welcome the parent, share the basic information, and pass along my husband's direct number. That evening, the parent called, and by the next day, a new client signed up for lessons. If I hadn't been present, that opportunity could have been lost. That moment opened my eyes to another dimension of helping: true help doesn't just cover; it multiplies.

My willingness created space for increase, not only in my husband's workload but in our household finances. It reminded me of Jesus' words in Matthew 5:41, "And if anyone forces you to go one mile, go with him two miles" (ESV). In its original context, Jesus was teaching His followers how to demonstrate kingdom love even in unjust situations. A Roman soldier could legally force a civilian to carry his load for one mile, but Jesus challenged His disciples to go farther than what was required. Why? Because love is revealed when we go beyond what is expected. That principle applies beautifully in marriage. Many times, we give the bare minimum of help in the areas we choose. But when we step into the places our husbands truly need support, even when it costs us something, we go the extra mile. That is where rest comes to him.

That is where love is felt more deeply. And often, that is where increase shows up.

Sometimes we think we are helping, but we are only giving what is easy for us to give. The real measure of help is found in the places where our husbands need covering, where they can breathe because we have stepped in. That is the field of intelligence we should learn to identify: not what feels convenient to us, but what strengthens him. And when you move in that place, your help carries the power to multiply.

Discovering Your Husband's Love Language

If you ask my husband what his love language is, he'll probably say one word: Tamminn. Gifts are nice, but if they don't include me, they don't land the same. If I were to put him on Dr. Chapman's Love Language scale, his favorite things would be quality time and acts of service (in a reverse sense). I didn't need a love language quiz to figure that out. I learned it by watching him, studying him, paying attention. He lights up when I take care of myself, with my hair done, skin glowing, eating right, working out, and taking vitamins, then he gets to take that all in by spending time with me. When I care for myself, it sends him a message that I'm whole, present, and well. That's not textbook 'acts of service', but it's his language.

Your husband has a language too. It may not fit into a clean category. It might not be one of the five love languages. It might be in the reversed sense, or it might be his own scale entirely. So, if you can't find him in the formula, ask God: "How does this man receive love?" and ask your husband. Pay attention. Don't just do what makes sense to you, do what connects with him. Because love, real love, requires understanding. God Himself has preferences:

- Obedience (John 14:15)
- Intimacy (James 4:8, Psalm 22:3)
- Thanksgiving and praise (Hebrews 13:15)
- Serving others as unto Him (Matthew 25:40)
- Sacrifice offered in love (Proverbs 3:9)

But we don't learn that by guessing. We learn it by knowing Him, spending time in His Word, listening for His voice, and watching how He responds. Your husband is the same. You won't always get it right. But love is not about perfection; it's about pursuit. The more you know him, the better you'll love him. The more you serve him with understanding, the more your home becomes a place of alignment and peace. Because submission isn't just about hierarchy, it's about humility, and love requires intentionality.

ACTION STEP: Ask him directly or observe his reactions. Speak his love language regularly, especially when you feel least like doing it.

3. Know His Conflict Style
Does he:
- Withdraw and go quiet?
- Lash out?
- Try to fix things quickly?
- Shut down?

Just like in battle, every soldier has a default reaction when tension arises. Some withdraw. Some explode. Some fix. Some avoid. As a wife, your goal isn't to criticize his response, but to understand it, and to respond with wisdom, not reaction. "A wise woman builds her home, but a foolish woman tears it down with her own hands." (Proverbs 14:1, NLT) Wisdom doesn't just react to what's happening. Wisdom watches, discerns, and then builds based on what she sees. Conflict is not always a sign that something is wrong; it's a sign that two people are still growing. The danger isn't conflict. It's when we handle it without understanding each other's wiring.

Questions to consider:
- Does your husband need time to process before talking?
- Does he feel disrespected when you raise your tone?
- Does he shut down when he feels criticized?
- Does he move into 'fix-it' mode when all you want is connection?

These are not flaws. These are clues. And clues lead to understanding.

Biblical Insights

David, a man after God's own heart, was also a man of passion and intensity. He didn't always handle conflict perfectly. He made impulsive decisions. He had moments of rage (like almost killing Nabal). He had seasons where he avoided hard conversations (like when Absalom rebelled). But he was also quick to repent, tender with God, and courageous in battle.

If your husband is wired like David. Deep, intense, sometimes reactive. Don't silence him, study him. Learn when to speak and when to stay quiet. Learn when he needs space and when he needs prayer. "The purposes of a man's heart are deep waters, but a man of understanding draws them out." (Proverbs 20:5, ESV). Your job isn't to change his war style, it's to help him sharpen it. You are his safe place and his intercessor. Be mindful of being too critical.

Other biblical examples:
- Absalom (2 Samuel 13–18): Avoider of confrontation. Carried bitterness silently. Shows the danger of unresolved offense.
- Joseph (Genesis 37–50): Quiet strength. Controlled emotions. Shows a model of emotional maturity and patience under pressure.

- Peter (John 18:10, Matthew 26:75): Impulsive but deeply loyal. Cut a man's ear off, then wept in repentance after denying Christ. A picture of passion being refined.

Each of these men had different conflict responses, and each required grace to grow. "A soft answer turns away wrath, but a harsh word stirs up anger." (Proverbs 15:1, ESV). Don't just guess how to handle conflict, ask God:

- How is my husband wired?
- What triggers him?
- What calms him?
- What grows him?

Conflict is not the enemy; confusion is. Understanding brings alignment. And when you understand his war style, you can love him more deeply through every battle. Because conflict is always an invitation for transformation.

WISDOM MOVE: Don't take his style personally. Learn to meet him in his space with patience, not pressure.

4. Know His Stress Triggers

Every man has a pressure point. A place where he feels the weight of expectation or the sting of inadequacy. As a wife, your spiritual intelligence includes knowing what triggers his stress. Ask him: "What usually makes you feel most pressured in life or marriage?" And then cover that area in prayer daily. It could be finances, failing at work, or not feeling respected at home. It could be being misunderstood or carrying too much responsibility. Moses cried out to God under the pressure of leading the people. He said, "I am not able to carry all this people alone; the burden is too heavy for me." (Numbers 11:14, ESV) Even a great leader can feel crushed under constant demands. When you understand what stresses your husband, you can support him with compassion instead of assumptions. You can truly be his helper, instead of being another weight.

5. Know His Dreams & Fears

Your husband may have both a vision for success and a fear of failure, even if he doesn't say it out loud. As his wife, you are called to help him cultivate the former and pray against the latter. Ask God: "What is my husband dreaming of that he's afraid to pursue?"

"What is he terrified might fail?" Then ask your husband with curiosity, not pressure. Understanding these helps you to pray with precision, encourage with insight, and support with intention. In Judges 6, Gideon was hiding in fear when the angel of the Lord called him a mighty warrior. His fear of failure was real, but so was the potential God saw in him. Sometimes your husband just needs someone to call out the warrior in him.

I remember going to breakfast with my husband one morning. We had this routine where we'd go to Panera Bread when he was free, just to sit, have coffee, and connect. During one of those

113

mornings, I simply asked him, "Baby, is there anything that you want to do? Any project you want to work on soon?" I was so in awe of how many things he shared with me, things he had been thinking about doing, dreams he had for our family, and where he saw us in the next few years. My heart was touched. I didn't want to forget a single thing. So, I bought him a journal to write down. He never used it, but you know what I did? I wrote the things down for him. Sometimes all it takes is one simple question to open a river of vision inside your husband. Even if he doesn't write it down or "make it plain," remember that you are one. So, when he tells you something, it's not just his vision. It's yours too. Write it down. Make it plain. Bring it before the Lord in prayer. Pray over it. Stand on it. Do what's required to help that vision come to pass. Because when you carry his vision, you are carrying part of your calling as a wife.

Testimony: The Slippers and the Story Behind Them

One of the fears I picked up over time came out in a way I didn't expect. My husband has always been particular about our kids walking barefoot on the cold floor. He didn't want them to get sick. He'd get visibly upset if he saw them without house slippers. At first, I thought it was over-the-top. I'd say things like, "They're just kids, they'll be fine. It's not that serious." It annoyed me at times because I didn't understand where it was coming from. But then, one day while my mother-in-law was visiting us, she shared something that really got to my heart. She told me about my husband's younger brother who died suddenly as a child. The doctors never figured out the exact cause, but my husband suspected pneumonia. What struck me most was when she mentioned that our son looks just like my husband's baby brother. And in that moment, something clicked. My husband never said it out loud, but he was carrying the trauma of that loss in his subconscious. Every time he saw our son barefoot on the cold floor, something inside him triggered. It wasn't just about health, it was about grief, protection, and unhealed pain.

From that moment on, I stopped making a big deal about the slippers. I had insight, and with that insight came compassion. Instead of reacting, I responded with grace. And you know what? Over time, he stopped being as strict about it. I don't know if it was because I stopped fighting it, or because God brought healing through my understanding. But there was a release for both of us. This is why knowing his fears matters. What looks like control could be unresolved pain. What looks like overprotection could be hidden grief. Ask God for insight. Ask questions. You may discover that the thing that frustrates you is rooted in something sacred.

6. Know His Spiritual Temperature

Where is your husband with God? This question isn't to shame or grade him, it's to help you walk in alignment and intercession. Is he on fire? Is he coasting? Is he wrestling with doubt or shame? Does he connect with God through worship, nature, teaching, or silence? In John 21, after denying Jesus, Peter's spiritual confidence was low. But Jesus met him with restoration, not rebuke. He asked Peter three times, "Do you love Me?" and then called him back into purpose. God didn't throw Peter away; He re-lit the flame. Knowing your husband's spiritual temperature helps you: pray wisely, encourage gently, and support without nagging. Sometimes he needs a reminder, not of what he's not doing, but of who he truly is. Ask God to help you see right. and when needed, ask your husband honestly: "How's your heart with God lately?" Then listen, without fixing.

As you learn to see your husband with fresh vision, you'll also discover the importance of adjusting with grace, because love not only sees clearly, but it also adapts wisely. We will explore the art of adaptability in the next chapter.

Prayer

Father, reveal my husband to me the way You see him. Help me to love what You love about him and be patient with what You're still working on. Purify my heart from assumptions, resentment, or fear, so I can see him through your eyes. Give me spiritual insight, not to control him, but to cover him. Help me listen more, assume less, and serve with joy, not pressure. Where I've missed his heart, give me fresh eyes. Where I've spoken from pain, give me gentle words. Make me a safe place for him. Make me a student of his soul, not just a partner in life, but a woman of understanding. Let my pursuit of him be pure. In Jesus' name, Amen.

Journal Reflection

What area of my husband's inner world feels like a mystery to me?

What can I ask or observe this week to learn more?

Do I give him the same grace to be known that I desire for myself?

Am I approaching my husband with a pure heart, or a filtered one clouded by disappointment, frustration, or fear?

Weekly Check-In Mission

- Start a simple weekly check-in routine:
- Ask: "How are you doing spiritually, emotionally, and physically?"
- Share your own answers honestly
- End with a short prayer or word of encouragement

TEN

THE ART OF ADAPTABILITY

When the Battle Plan Changes

Every military operation includes a contingency plan. Why? Because conditions shift. Terrain changes. And even the most well-researched strategies must bend to the reality of the moment. Marriage works the same way. You may have walked in with expectations, about roles, routines, or how love should look. But when life changes (and it will), your ability to adapt can either protect your peace or magnify your frustration.

This chapter is about spiritual flexibility; how to hold your mission steady while letting your methods evolve. Adaptability isn't about losing yourself. It's about posturing your spirit like Christ. Humble, surrendered, and fully yielded to the Father's will.

Positioned to Pivot: The Silent Strength of Adaptability

Adaptability is not about giving up. It's about growing up. It's choosing to respond to change with reverence instead of resistance. It's trusting that God's detours still lead to destiny, even when they disrupt your comfort or expectations. One of the greatest pivots I've had to make as a wife and woman came when I moved to the United States. I had a plan. I was pursuing a bachelor's degree in Banking and Finance when I met my husband. I had ambition and clear career goals. Back in Jamaica, Finance seemed like the smart path, stable, respected, and full of potential.

But truthfully, it was never my passion. I didn't choose it because I loved it. I chose it because it felt safe, and my dream was always to work at Scotia Bank. Deep down, my heart had always been drawn to something else. Fields like psychology, social work, and counseling were what stirred my spirit. I just didn't think they were realistic options at the time. But when I moved to the U.S., everything began to shift.

My husband was in the U.S. on an O-1 visa for individuals with extraordinary ability in a specific field. As his spouse, I was granted an O-3 visa. It allowed me to live here legally, go to school, volunteer, and minister, but I couldn't earn an income. That limitation was heavy. I had spent years preparing for a professional life, only to find myself unable to work. Still, I didn't give up. I went back to school and pursued my master's degree in clinical social work. For the first time, it felt like I was stepping into something that aligned deeply with how God had wired me. The program gave me formal training in therapeutic work, including therapy for individuals, couples, and families, as well as those facing complex mental health challenges. It reflected everything I was naturally passionate about: healing, restoration, emotional insight, and family systems. Finally, I felt like my purpose and my education were finally pointing in the same direction. And everything around me confirmed it.

The way God opened doors for my graduate program felt miraculous. The favor, the timing, it all seemed to say, "This is it." But after graduation, even with the degree in hand, the same limitation remained: I still couldn't work. That reality led me into a hard place. Not because I didn't love being a wife and mother, I absolutely did. I cherished taking my children to school, being there for their doctor's visits, showing up for recitals and school events. I wouldn't trade those experiences for anything. But I also desired to walk in the career I thought I was now prepared for.

And when every door stayed shut, I began to grieve quietly. Deeply. I felt blocked. Stuck. And at times, discouraged enough to question my worth. But God didn't leave me in the dark. In my personal prayer time, He began speaking clearly. And He didn't stop there. One day, my sister in the faith who knew about my visa limitations but had no idea what God had been whispering to me or how I was wrestling, prayed for me and said: "The Lord says, you work for Him" It stopped me in my tracks. That was the exact phrase God had already been speaking to me privately. She didn't know that part. She didn't know how much I had been grieving or questioning. But God did. And He confirmed, once again, that I wasn't on pause. I was on assignment. I was being positioned.

God didn't just carry my family. He established us in His order. We lacked nothing. Through God's abundant provision and divine order, my husband has been blessed to fully take care of our family without needing my income to make ends meet, while supporting all my dreams. It wasn't the plan I expected, but it was the covering God had already prepared. Caring for my home, raising my children, and tending to my husband has always been one of the most rewarding callings of my life.

What looked to some like limitation in being unable to work outside the home was, in truth, God's intentional placement. In that hidden place, He was sharpening me. For twelve years as a wife and ten years as a mother, God was preparing me for the very work I'm now doing beyond the four walls of my home. The love, patience, and strength it took to nurture my family became the very training ground for what I now do in helping women and families. I didn't know it then, but every prayer whispered over my children, every moment of support for my husband, and every sacrifice made within my home was equipping me to minister to others.

Today, I see clearly that the same grace that sustained me in my home is the grace God now multiplies through me to restore families and help women thrive in their identity, marriage, and motherhood. And now I know: every class, every insight, every part of my social work education has found purpose. God was training me not just for clinical practice, but for Kingdom impact. He was shaping a voice for the broken, a heart for marriages, and a calling rooted in wisdom and truth. And the things I thought I'd use in another setting? He's now using through me, in ministry, in mentorship, in this book, and in every family, He allows me to speak into. Sometimes, the pivot isn't away from purpose; it's the path into it. And sometimes, God closes the doors you wanted, to open the ones you didn't even know were yours.

The Art of Adaptability

Some wives fear that if they "bend," they're being walked over. But biblical submission isn't about being inert or voiceless, it's about being Spirit-led and situationally aware. The goal isn't to control every variable. The goal is to respond to change without compromising your identity or mission. Adaptability looks like:

- Gracefully shifting when life throws curveballs
- Giving your husband space to grow, change, or even struggle
- Letting go of rigid timelines or comparison traps
- Staying anchored in God while surrendering your personal agenda

WHEN ADAPTABILITY IS NEEDED MOST

1. *Where There is Transitions & Life Changes*
   New job, new baby, move, health crisis, spiritual dry season, loss

TACTICAL MOVE: Don't panic. Pause. Pray. Adjust expectations. Ask, "What does obedience look like right now?"

2. *Where There is Unmet Expectations*
   You thought he'd lead prayer more. You assumed you'd be more emotionally connected by now. You expected him to understand your needs without spelling them out.

TACTICAL MOVE: Choose clarity over resentment. Communicate with grace, not assumptions. Grieve what's unmet but don't weaponize it.

3. *Where There is Spiritual Mismatch or Delays*
   You're growing spiritually faster than he is. He seems stagnant, or uninterested in God.

TACTICAL MOVE: Don't force or pressure. Stay prayerful. Lead by example. Trust God's timeline, not yours.

Biblical Wives Who Adapted
Sarah left her homeland and waited on a promise. She teaches us to trust when timelines stretch.

Ruth embraced an entirely new culture and life. She reminds us that faithfulness in uncertainty leads to fruitfulness.

Abigail stayed honorable in a dishonorable marriage. Her discernment protected her household and positioned her for promotion.

Esther walked into a palace she didn't choose to fulfill a purpose she couldn't have planned.

Mary, the mother of Jesus, embraced a divine assignment she never asked for. She teaches us to carry promise in silence and faith.

God isn't asking you to be a statue. He's calling you to be a Spirit-led soldier. Adaptability doesn't mean you're lost, it means you're being led, and in the Kingdom, flexibility is a part of the rhythm of faith. Be encouraged not to fear the pivot when change comes, because the steps of the righteous are ordered by the Lord. Even when the path feels unfamiliar, the Word of God remains a lamp unto your feet and a light unto your path (Psalm 119:105). You are never walking alone. His presence is with you, guiding you into what He has already prepared. Trust that His plans for your life will always prevail, even when they look different than what you expected. And as you walk with confidence in Him, this posture will strengthen your ability to be a steady support for your husband, leading gently from the rear; a role we will look at more deeply in the next chapter.

Prayer
Father, Thank You for being faithful in every season. When things shift suddenly, help me to lean on You, not my own understanding. Teach me to adapt without losing my identity or my posture of submission. Help me respond with obedience like Sarah, Ruth, Abigail, Esther, Mary, and like You've taught me to. I trust You with the pivot. I trust You with the outcome. In Jesus' name, amen.

Journal Reflection
Where is God asking you to adapt right now?

Are you grieving the change—or submitting to the shift?

The 3-Point Pivot

When something doesn't go as planned this week:

1. Pause — Acknowledge the shift.
2. Pray — Ask, "God, what's my role here?"
3. Pivot — Adjust your words, schedule, or strategy in love.

ELEVEN

LEADING FROM THE REAR STRENGHT OF SUPPORT

Leadership in the Shadows

In the military, some of the most powerful leaders aren't the ones charging in front. They're the ones coordinating from the rear: ensuring every move is supported, every resource is in place, and every strategy is covered. As a wife, God may not always call you to lead visibly in your marriage. But that doesn't mean you're not leading. You lead from the spiritual rear through prayer, encouragement, quiet strength, and strategic support. This is one of the most potent positions in the Kingdom.

Your submission doesn't cancel your leadership. It redirects it through humility and wisdom. When you "lead from the rear," you:

- Influence without manipulation
- Serve without silencing your identity
- Encourage without enabling
- Strengthen your husband through spiritual, emotional, and practical support

True support is filled with divine strength. It builds something in your husband that pressure never could.

My Role as COO — His Strength Behind the Scenes

About three years ago, during a marriage conference my husband and I hosted at our church while leading the marriage ministry, we invited a trusted couple in the faith, Reverend Nicholas Robertson and his lovely wife, Lady Danielle. They have done tremendous work and continue to be a consistent source of wisdom for marriages and families. That day, part of Reverend Robertson's message gave me language for a spiritual reality I had been living but hadn't quite articulated. He spoke about the roles within marriage in a way that compared the husband to a CEO and the wife to a COO, or Chief Operating Officer. I may not remember his exact wording, but the essence of it was clear. That illustration became an 'aha' moment for me and has continued to shape how I view the order and partnership within my home.

My husband balances the responsibility of providing for our family with remaining present at home and a steady commitment to serving in God's house. And while he's out building and leading, I hold things down at home. I manage the schedule, care for our children, handle school and doctor appointments, and strive to ensure that peace, not pressure greets him when he walks through the door. I try to create an atmosphere of warmth, order, and rest. But hear me: I don't say this to make it sound easy or perfect. I'm not always nailing it. There have been chaotic days, tearful moments, and seasons when I was figuring it out as I went. But over time, I began to see this role not as a burden, but as a strategic post. One I've grown to honor.

I didn't always understand the weight of this assignment. In fact, there was a time I felt almost embarrassed to only do that. When other parents in our school district would ask, "What do you do?" I used to shrink. I'd quickly blurt out, "Well, I have a master's degree in social work..." even when no one asked. I wanted them to know I had done "something," even if I wasn't using my degree the way I thought I would. Looking back, I realize I was wrestling with insecurity. I didn't fully understand the power of my position. But God did. And He gently corrected me. One day, He whispered: "You have the most important job on this side of creation. You're raising world-changers. You're stewarding My legacy. You're not just holding down the house. You're holding up purpose. And the fruit of that is undeniable."

No, it's not always glamorous. Yes, it takes strategic planning, sacrifice, and a whole lot of grace, but there is reward. There is joy. There is purpose. The atmosphere of your home will testify. The strength of your husband will reflect it, and growth in your children will reveal it. Marriages do work, but they don't work by accident. They flourish through faith, intention, and obedience. And the beautiful thing is, when you show up and steward your part, God shows up too. He breathes on your efforts. He increases you in grace. And He makes sure the harvest is always greater than the seed.

Leading from the Rear is a Prophetic Position

As wives and helpers, we carry a sacred assignment. We are not just covering our husbands in prayer; we are often receiving divine intelligence for the mission ahead. God will reveal things to us that He may not reveal to our husbands first. Not because we are more spiritual, but because our position requires that level of discernment and readiness. We see this pattern throughout Scripture:

- The angel visited Mary before Joseph received confirmation in a dream (Matthew 1:18–25).
- God spoke to Samson's mother before He gave the message to his father (Judges 13).

These women were entrusted with revelation, and strategic insight that would shape the destiny of their families. Why? Because they were helpers by divine design. And help isn't just physical, it's prophetic. It's spiritual and strategic.

But with revelation comes responsibility. Can God trust you to steward the insight He gives for your household? Are you a woman of integrity, honor, and restraint? Are you able to carry a word from Heaven without manipulating outcomes or weaponizing what you hear? When you go to your husband and say, "I believe the Lord said…"—can he trust you? That trust is not built in moments of prophecy alone. It's built in your everyday posture. It's cultivated through humility, maturity, and restraint. Over time, what you share becomes trustworthy, not because you're persuasive, but because you've proven to be submitted to God and not driven by control. That's what gives your voice spiritual weight. Not volume, not title, but trust. This is the quiet strength of the rear guard. The wife who is both an intercessor and a spiritual advisor in her home.

And here's something even more profound: The Bible calls the Holy Spirit our Helper (John 14:26). And the Bible also calls the wife a helper (Genesis 2:18). That's not a coincidence. The word used in Genesis 2:18—"ezer"—is the same Hebrew root used in Scripture to describe God Himself as a helper, protector, and deliverer (Psalm 33:20, Deuteronomy 33:29). This word does not imply inferiority, it implies strength. So, when God said, "It is not good that the man should be alone; I will make him a helper fit for him." (Genesis 2:18, ESV), He wasn't saying, "I'll give him someone to do the chores." He was saying, "I'm going to give him a powerful, strategically designed partner who will help carry out Heaven's assignment."

You are not a background extra in your home. You are not a tagalong to your husband's purpose. You are not optional to the success of your family's mission. You are part of the divine strategy. You are called to discern, to intercede, to build, and to protect. You are called to lead, even if it's from the unseen places. And your influence doesn't come from being loud or dominant, it comes from being spiritually aligned and divinely positioned.

Hired by Heaven — Your Assignment Matters

There is one truth that must stay anchored in your heart: You were hired by Heaven. You work for God. Think of it this way: if you worked at a company and had a clear role to fulfill, you'd show up with purpose because you know your contribution impacts the greater mission. You'd understand that if you dropped the ball, someone else would feel it. The same is true in marriage. Heaven has a vision for your household, and you were chosen to carry part of that assignment. You are not just helping your husband; you are partnering with God to fulfill Heaven's plan.

And here's the weight of it, prophetically and practically: In military operations, when a soldier abandons their post or fails to carry out their assigned role, it can jeopardize the entire mission. It exposes the unit to vulnerability. Gaps open. Communication breaks down. Lives are lost. Victory is delayed. A single act of neglect in the field can significantly impact the outcome for the entire battalion.

The same principle applies in the spirit. When a wife who has been spiritually positioned as an intercessor, and a helper refuses to show up, the ripple effect is real. It doesn't just impact her. It impacts the children. It affects the emotional climate of the home. It burdens the husband. It opens the door for confusion and disunity to enter. Sometimes it even puts pressure on him to carry things God never meant for him to carry alone. And when this happens long enough, Heaven, like any good Commander, may have to reassign the mission. Not because God is punishing you, but because the mission still matters. If one soldier won't rise, the Commander must raise another.

What is required of us as wives goes beyond convenience or personal preference. It touches the very mission of the union. Mordecai told Esther:

> "For if you remain silent at this time, relief and deliverance for the Jews will arise from another place, but you and your father's family will perish. And who knows but that you have come to your royal position for such a time as this?" (Esther 4:14, NIV)

In other words, if she refused her assignment, God would raise up another. The same principle applies in our homes: the assignment of your marriage is bigger than you as an individual and bigger than you as a couple. We see this truth echoed in the life of Saul. Though chosen as king, his disobedience caused God to remove him from his position:

> "But now your kingdom will not endure; the Lord has sought out a man after his own heart and appointed him ruler of his people, because you have not kept the Lord's command." (1 Samuel 13:14, NIV)

Later, Scripture makes it even clearer:

> "Because you have rejected the word of the Lord, he has rejected you as king." (1 Samuel 15:23, NIV)

In the same way, if we continually neglect the mandate God places on us as wives, He can set us aside and raise up another to carry it forward. This does not mean God rejects us as His daughters, but there is a sobering difference between being His child and being His servant. Obedience ensures we remain in position, not only as loved daughters, but also as faithful stewards of the assignments entrusted to us, because servants can be fired.

Have you ever seen someone remarry and suddenly they seem to thrive in ways they never did in the previous marriage? Sometimes, that's because the assignment was forfeited, and God raised up someone else who would steward it with honor. This isn't a call to fear, it's a call to purpose. It may sound harsh, but it's also filled with mercy: You are still here. You are still called. And your yes still matters. Don't be like Vashti, who refused to come when the King called. Be like Esther, who walked in obedience, strategy, and favor. Esther's influence came not just from beauty, but from submission to divine timing. She fasted, prayed, and approached her assignment with wisdom. And through her obedience, a nation was delivered. You may not be standing before a Persian king, but you are standing in your home with Heaven's authority. Don't underestimate your reach. Your tone, presence, spiritual discernment, and obedience can shift the climate of your entire household and generations. You're not just a wife. You're an appointed ambassador.

As you lead with obedience and authority, don't forget the companion that carries you through every season—joy. In the next chapter we'll talk about how to keep joy alive in the journey.

Prayer

Father, thank You for calling me, positioning me, and equipping me to be a helper not just to my husband, but to Your vision for our family. Help me lead from the rear with wisdom, not resentment. Let me be spiritually sensitive, emotionally grounded, and prophetically sharp. Teach me to be trustworthy with revelation, gentle with correction, and strong in encouragement. Guard my heart from insecurity and comparison. Let my posture remain pure so that I may see You clearly and discern what You're doing in my household. I declare that I am not behind; I am in divine alignment. I lead well, I support well, and I will steward this assignment with excellence. In Jesus' name, Amen.

Journal Reflection

Where have I been shrinking back from my role as a spiritual support in my home through discouragement, fear, or distraction?

How can I become more sensitive to the Holy Spirit's leading as a wife and helper?

Have I been silencing my voice out of fear or frustration, or am I learning how to speak with wisdom and strength?

What would it look like this week to embrace my position as Heaven's ambassador in my home with fresh confidence and grace?

Is there an area of my marriage or household where God is calling me to step back into position because the mission still matters?

TWELVE

MORALE MAINTENANCE KEEPING JOY IN THE JOURNEY

Joy is a Battle Strategy

In war, morale isn't a luxury; it's a lifeline. Soldiers with low morale are more likely to give up, turn on each other, or lose focus. But when morale is high, when hope is alive, even a weary soldier can stay in the fight. In the same way, marriage is spiritual warfare, and joy is the morale of your home. Joy is your frontline defense against bitterness, burnout, and breakdown. It keeps your heart soft in hard seasons and your home connected in the midst of chaos. This chapter is your reminder that joy isn't just a feeling; it's fuel. It's a spiritual weapon, a sacred strategy, and it must be fought for, protected, and intentionally pursued, especially in long battles.

I'm not talking about shallow happiness. I'm talking about the deep, soul-satisfying kind of joy that comes from honoring God's order. Where love is expressed, respect is practiced, and righteousness is pursued. When a wife chooses to align her heart and actions with what God says, when she hungers for righteousness in her marriage, she will be filled. Filled with peace. Filled with strength. Filled with the kind of joy that holds a house together.

Why Marital Joy Matters

Joy doesn't ignore problems; it sustains you through them. It gives you:

- Emotional resilience when things feel heavy
- Perspective when the days feel routine
- A reason to stay soft and connected in hard seasons

Without joy, love starts to feel like a job. But with joy, even tough seasons feel like a team effort. And here's the good news: joy is not something you have to conjure up on your own. It's something Heaven invites you to ask for. Jesus Himself said, "Ask, and you will receive, that your joy may be full." (John 16:24, ESV). This isn't a casual offer. It's a divine promise. Sometimes, we don't ask because we think joy must be earned, or that it's a reward for good behavior. But Jesus ties joy to asking, because joy in your soul, and in your marriage, is a sign that you are living in alignment with Heaven's heart. So, ask. Ask for joy to be restored. Ask for laughter to return. Ask for the delight that once brought you together to bubble up again. Joy is your strength. It is your fuel. It is part of your inheritance as a daughter of God, and as a wife who hungers and thirsts for things to be right, not just with your husband, but your whole life.

A Biblical Example: Abraham and Sarah

Even when circumstances seemed laughable, Abraham and Sarah were promised joy. In Genesis 18, Sarah laughed when she overheard the Lord say she would have a son in her old age. Her laugh wasn't one of excitement. It was disbelief. She was worn out. The timeline was past due. And hope felt distant. But later, that same laugh became a sound of fulfillment. When Isaac was born, she said, "God has brought me laughter, and everyone who hears will laugh with me." (Genesis 21:6, NIV)

What began in weariness ended in joy. Sometimes joy begins as a whisper in the dark, a flicker of hope in a tired heart. But when God fulfills His promise, laughter returns. Even if you're in a season of waiting, trust that joy is not lost; it's loading. Sometimes God waits until joy would look ridiculous... and then He delivers. Because He wants the laughter in your home to carry testimony. Joy isn't always loud, but when it arrives, everyone around you will feel it. Joy is a fruit of the Spirit, but it doesn't grow by accident. It thrives where the heart stays aligned with Heaven and refuses to bow to circumstances.

What Drains Joy in Marriage

Before we discuss cultivating joy, let's examine what often drains it. Joy doesn't usually disappear all at once. It fades slowly when maintenance replaces mission—when we stop building toward purpose and start simply keeping things running, when assumptions replace communication, and when criticism replaces gratitude. Here are a few common joy-drainers:

- Unexpressed or unclear expectations that go unmet
- Harsh or hurried communication
- Lack of gratitude for what's already present
- Unbalanced responsibilities over time
- Busyness that replaces intentional connection
- Emotional wounds that are ignored instead of addressed

The enemy loves to use small irritations to erode joy. He knows if he can't steal your love, he'll try to steal your laughter. And once joy is gone, everything starts to feel heavier than it really is. Sometimes joy is leaking, not because something major is wrong, but because the little foxes have been left unchallenged. Those foxes—resentment, assumptions, busyness, unspoken disappointments will keep gnawing until you make a decision to guard what's sacred. Joy doesn't thrive in survival mode. It needs space, intention, and regular maintenance. Not because you're failing, but because you're still growing.

A Biblical Insight: Expectations Reframed

When expectations are never communicated, they easily become weapons of disappointment. We assume our spouse "should just know," and then punish them silently when they don't. However, a healthy connection is not built on assumptions; it's built on honest exchange. And honest exchange requires courage, grace, and patience. Instead of nurturing silent frustration, speak in love. Don't assume malice where there may be misunderstanding. Take ownership of your heart's needs but stay rooted in gratitude for what is already present.

We see this tension in the story of Martha and Mary (Luke 10:38–42). Martha had expectations, possibly unspoken, that her sister would be helping with the preparations. But when she finally voiced her frustration to Jesus, His response was not a rebuke of her heart, but a redirection of her focus. Mary had chosen what mattered most in that moment: presence over work. The unmet expectation wasn't inherently wrong, but it had to be surrendered. I've learned that unmet expectations are invitations.

- Invitations to check our motives
- Invitations to revisit how we communicate
- Invitations to return to the heart of what truly matters

When joy starts to fade in your marriage, ask yourself: Is this really a failure on his part, or is this a place where my heart needs to be realigned with God's? Joy flourishes in truth, not perfect circumstances, but truthful, grace-filled connection. Sometimes, God has to gently pull us out of our expectations so we can see the deeper thing He's revealing: the heart.

I remember a time when my daughter was in preschool and had an assignment to create something for school. I was exhausted that night, so I left the project in my husband's hands and went to bed, trusting that he would help her finish it. The next morning, I woke up early to take her to school, and when I looked at the project, my heart sank. He had done the wrong thing. I was frustrated. It wasn't what the assignment required, and now she would have to turn it in late. I felt overwhelmed, disappointed, and upset. But my cousin happened to be there that morning, and as I explained why I was so frustrated, she gently said, "But at least he stayed up and tried. He stayed up the whole night to make something." And in that moment, my heart softened. She was right. He may have missed the mark in execution, but his heart was present. His effort was love. He didn't ignore the task; he stayed up into the early morning hours trying to get it done.

I learned a valuable lesson about marriage: sometimes we need to learn to read past the result and into the heart. It's not about lowering standards. It's about recognizing love when it looks different from how we imagined. Sometimes, your husband will get it wrong but still tried with everything he had. Learn to decode his heart. Don't miss the offering because it didn't come wrapped the way you expected. Grace doesn't mean we stop communicating expectations, but it does mean we slow down enough to see the motive before we criticize the method.

TACTICAL JOY-BUILDING STRATEGIES

Joy doesn't just happen. It must be protected and pursued. These simple yet powerful strategies will help you safeguard the joy in your home, especially during seasons that feel routine, overwhelming, or uninspiring.

1. Celebrate Small Wins

Marriage doesn't need massive milestones to feel meaningful. Sometimes, the most sacred victories are the quiet ones, the "we made it through this week" moments, the bedtime giggles with the kids, the unspoken looks that say, "I'm still with you." Celebrate those. Your celebration is a declaration that the little things matter, and joy multiplies where gratitude flows.

2. Schedule Joy on Purpose

In a world that constantly reminds us to prioritize self-care, let's not forget the joy of intentionally caring for one another. Scheduling joy in your marriage is not just about what makes you happy; it's about noticing and creating moments that bring life to your husband too. What brings him joy? What helps him reset and feel seen?

My husband is an outgoing person. His favorite thing to do is spend time with me. For him, Friday night date night is sacred. It gives him energy, joy, and connection. There have been nights when I was exhausted. When the last thing I wanted to do was get dressed and go out, but I went, not out of obligation, but out of love. I've learned that when I choose to sow joy into him, I'm tending to the garden of our covenant. And the beautiful part is that, often, going out was just what my soul needed to reset after my week.

This is what love does. It doesn't keep score. It doesn't wait for conditions to be ideal. It gives and trusts God with the return. As you reflect this week, ask yourself:

- What makes my husband feel deeply connected?

- What simple joy can I create to refresh his heart?
- How can I make space for joy even in a busy season?

Your version of joy might look like grocery runs together, long walks at dusk, spontaneous movie nights on the couch, or late-night pillow talks. Whatever it looks like, be intentional. Protect the moments that connect your hearts.

3. Speak Life Daily

Encouragement is like fuel. A simple "I'm proud of you," or "Thank you for…" can shift the atmosphere of your home in ways you may not immediately see, but Heaven sees it, and your husband feels it. Sometimes we want more, not because our husbands are doing nothing, but because we're craving something more specific, more intimate, more personal.

There was a time I shared with my husband that I wanted more attention, not because he wasn't present, but because I longed for a deeper connection to the things that make me feel seen. He was doing a great job providing for our family and showing up in all the expected ways. But part of me felt like I wanted him to do a little more, not just for us, but for me. And after expressing that to him, the Holy Spirit interrupted my thoughts with a gentle but firm truth: "You have expectations, Tamminn, but how about thanking him more for the things he is already doing? Even the responsibilities he's expected to fulfill, thank him for those." That truth shook me. So, I started doing just that. I thanked my husband more intentionally:

- Thank you for being a good father to our children.
- Thank you for being the best husband
- Thank you for taking such good care of our family
- Thank you for making us feel safe

- Thank you for paying the bills.
- Thank you for checking in on me throughout the day.
- Thank you for caring about my health.
- Thank you for making decisions with me in mind.
- Thank you for leaving the last drop of coffee for me.

I have developed a habit of thanking my husband daily. The more I thank him, the more I truly see him. The more I thank him, the more I recognize God's hand working through him. The more I thank him, the more I see how blessed our family really is. And as I thank him for shepherding us so well, I see the Lord, our true Shepherd, manifesting in our home every day. The more I thank my husband, the more I thank God.

That simple shift changed the atmosphere in me and in our home. It made him feel honored and seen, but it was doing far more in me than I could have ever imagined.

Then the Lord took it deeper. He reminded me of when Jesus fed the five thousand. He didn't wait for abundance to be thankful. He lifted what little was there — five loaves and two fish — and He gave thanks (Matthew 14:13–21). That thanksgiving triggered multiplication. And the Holy Spirit said to me: "If you don't have words of life to bless where you are, you're not ready for where you're asking to go."

That moment wrecked me in the best way. We say we want more, but if we can't steward the seed, how will we carry the harvest? If I can't bless what looks small, am I truly ready for more? That was a moment of awakening. If I wanted to see more love from my husband, I needed to first bless the love that was already present. And can I tell you something? When I honor my husband, I feel like the most loved and satisfied wife in the world. I've discovered that joy flows where gratitude lives. Just one look at him still makes my heart skip a beat. After twelve years together, I find myself still missing him the moment he leaves the room. Each day, I discover that I can love him more, need him more, and treasure his presence more than I ever thought possible. I am still captivated by my husband.

Before the end of every day, there are three things I look forward to — second only to my time with God. I long to hear the giggles and laughter of my children, to sink into a long, hot shower, and to rest against the steady vibration of my husband's heartbeat. These three simple joys steady me, remind me how blessed I am, and fill me before I close my eyes at night.

Here's your challenge: Go seven days without criticizing. Just thank, honor, and observe what changes. Bless what looks small. Speak life over what feels lacking. Multiply joy by multiplying gratitude. Because when your words become a well of life, joy has a place to rise again.

4. Laugh Together Again

Humor heals. It disarms tension and strengthens connection. Find what makes your husband laugh, not just a smile, but that deep-belly kind of laugh. For my husband, that's Jamaican comedy. There's something about those classic skits, especially the ones with Oliver Samuels, that unlock pure joy for him. He'll laugh until he cries. And to be honest, I didn't realize how important this was for our marriage until the world shut down during the pandemic in 2020. While others were overwhelmed by fear, grief, and isolation, our home was filled with joy, joy that carried us through. We were quarantined, yes, but we were also reconnected. We spent late nights watching comedy, reliving memories, and just laughing until our stomachs hurt. Sometimes it was those old Oliver Samuels skits. Other nights, it was a Renaissance movie about kingdoms and wars—my husband's other favorite genre. And every time he laughed; it reminded me: joy is worth protecting.

Those moments of laughter became anchors. They reminded us that no matter what was happening outside, we had peace inside our home. That's something I'll never trade. I encourage you to discover what makes your husband laugh. Create those moments on purpose. Don't wait until life settles down. Laughter isn't just a byproduct of a good marriage; it's a builder of one. And don't worry if you're the one initiating. When you sow joy into your husband's heart, you are also sowing joy into your home. The Holy Spirit, your divine Helper, will make sure it multiplies back to you. Marriage is about mutual joy, but sometimes it starts with intentional sowing. So, laugh again. Watch something funny together. Reminisce. Dance in the kitchen. Share the jokes you think are silly. Play the music that gets you both giggling. Whatever it is, choose joy. Your joy matters. Not just for you, but for the health of your marriage, the strength of your spirit, and the example you set for those watching your love unfold. Keep joy in the journey, it's one of your most powerful weapons.

A Warning from Scripture: When Joy is Dismissed

There's a sobering example in Scripture that reveals just how dangerous it is to dismiss joy in marriage, and it comes from the life of King David and his wife Michal. In 2 Samuel 6, David is bringing the Ark of the Covenant back to Jerusalem. It's a historic and holy moment, one of profound spiritual significance. David, overwhelmed with passion and reverence, begins to dance before the Lord with all his might. He's not performing for people, he's worshiping in freedom, stripped of pride, moving in pure joy before God. But Michal, his wife, looks out the window, sees David dancing, and despises him in her heart. She criticizes his joy, and dishonor him in his worship. Instead of celebrating the presence of God returning to their city, she mocks the very moment that Heaven was celebrating. David responds by reaffirming that his praise was for the Lord, not for her approval. And the Scripture closes that scene with this haunting line: "And Michal the daughter of Saul had no child to the day of her death" (2 Samuel 6:23, ESV).

Her barrenness wasn't just physical; it was the result of spiritual misalignment. She failed to recognize the beauty and power of joy in worship, in love, and in the presence of God. This connects back to what we discussed in the chapter two on *The Wars and the Bride*. When Adam and Eve disobeyed God, dishonor entered their union, and Scripture says the woman's desire would be contrary to her husband (Genesis 3:16). Eve produced physical children, but she and Adam could no longer be fruitful and multiply in the fullness of God's design. In the same way, Michal dishonored her husband by dismissing his joy in worship. Again, Amos 3:3 reminds us, "Can two walk together unless they are agreed?" If David and Michal could not even agree on worshiping the God of their salvation, then what could they truly produce together? The consequence of their misalignment is recorded as her barrenness.

There's a lesson here for us as wives: Never despise your husband's joy—especially the joy that flows from his connection with God. It doesn't matter what his relationship with God looks like. Respect it, even if you feel like you're closer to God than he is. Even if he doesn't pray like you, worship like you, or read the Bible like you, honor the measure he does have. Michal didn't, and you see how her story ended. If something brings your husband peace, helps him unwind, makes him laugh, or allows him to express his heart freely before God, don't belittle it. Joy is a gift. And when it's honored, it multiplies. But when it's mocked, something dies. Let your home be a place that honors joy. When your husband laughs, celebrate it. When he worships, join him. When he enjoys something simple, let that moment breathe.

Because honoring his joy is part of honoring the man God made him to be.

While Joy is keeping your hearts alive, structure will keep your home in order. In the next chapter, we'll talk about the logistics of love and how managing the home front becomes an expression of love and stewardship.

Prayer

Father, thank You for the gift of laughter, the strength of joy, and the grace to enjoy one another through every season. Where we've grown weary, bring refreshing. Where we've lost connection, bring reconnection. Help us to celebrate more, complain less, and find beauty in the ordinary moments. Help me, Lord, to see my husband with a pure heart, through Your eyes. Let me not miss the joy You've placed right in front of me because I'm distracted by disappointment. Help me to protect the light in our home and to sow joy even when it feels small. Show me how to laugh again. Help me to build with gladness and honor the joy that strengthens our covenant. Let our home be filled with laughter that heals, gratitude that multiplies, and joy that reflects the beauty of Your presence. In Jesus' name, Amen.

Journal Reflection

What has been draining the joy in our home recently?

What simple practice can we implement this week to reconnect?

How can I become more intentional about scheduling joy?

When was the last time we laughed—really laughed—together?

Have I been guarding my heart with purity, or has frustration clouded my ability to see the good?

THIRTEEN

LOGISTICS OF LOVE
MANAGING THE HOME FRONT

Every Army Needs Logistics

In military operations, victory isn't just about bravery on the battlefield; it's about what happens behind the scenes. Without supply lines, communication systems, and coordinated support, even the strongest soldiers collapse. In marriage, your home is the command center, and how it's managed affects everything else. This chapter is about the logistics of love: the rhythm, routines, and responsibilities that keep your marriage and family running smoothly. Because love includes structure, stewardship, and service.

Love Needs Infrastructure

Love is not just a feeling. It's action, visible, practical, and intentional. God doesn't just love in theory; He demonstrates His love through strategy. Before we were even formed, He laid out a redemptive plan for our salvation. That's love in motion. Even within the Trinity, we see order and function: God the Father leads, God the Son redeems, and God the Holy Spirit empowers. There is unity, but also clarity. That same principle applies in marriage. Healthy marriages don't just thrive on prayer; they thrive on planning and executing:

- Who's doing what?
- Are our roles clear?
- Are we both carrying too much, or not enough?
- How are we creating peace in our space?

God is not the author of confusion. And your home should reflect His order.

THREE PILLARS OF HOME FRONT MANAGEMENT

1. Communication & Clarity

This may look like:

- Weekly check-ins on schedules, needs, and concerns
- Clear roles
- Respecting each other's workload

Some couples thrive with visible task lists and shared calendars. Others, over time, develop a quiet rhythm. A flow of mutual understanding that doesn't require a rigid system. In our home, for example, we don't have chore charts stuck on the fridge. But we have a rhythm, and we pivot, and we support. I usually cook, and my husband cleans up after. My husband usually does the laundry, and I fold it, but on some days, he may start the laundry, and I'll finish it because he has to return to work.

A few months ago, though, he said he would fold, and I should do the laundry because I was slacking on folding. At first, I felt some type of way. How dare he think I wasn't folding fast enough? I even told him I didn't like what he said. But as I started to load the washer, I came to my senses. This is a sweet switch! I can't stand folding laundry—that's why it always takes me so long to get it done. Here I was making a big deal out of something that actually worked in my favor, but guess who did both washing and folding most of the summer?... Me! Since my husband had a busier summer schedule, I didn't wait for him to come home and do it. I covered him...And guess who has been doing it all since September?... My husband! Since I'm on crunch time with this book, he's been covering me. That's a part of our rhythm.

I typically do school drop-off and pick-up, but if I'm on the road or at an appointment, I communicate: "Babe, I'm running late. Can you get the kids?" That's clarity too. It's not about micromanagement, it's about mutual awareness and flexibility. That's what makes a household thrive. I've naturally taken on the responsibilities of managing doctors' appointments, paying bills, and coordinating school meetings. These are areas I flow in easily and handle without being asked. They've become part of how I serve and support our family. It's a part of my role as COO.

My husband, on the other hand, works almost every day! He ensures our finances are stable, the gas tank is full, and the cars are clean and ready to go, among other things. If I'm honest, sometimes it feels like the load is 80/20, sometimes in my direction, sometimes in his. But that's how we flow. We stay aware, communicate often, and adjust based on the season we're in. We've learned to lean into our natural strengths, not to create strict roles, but to create harmony. These practical responsibilities are more than just tasks; they're an expression of love, service, and unity in motion.

And even if there's no shared family schedule posted on the fridge, I've learned to keep one for myself. As a wife and mother, this helps me ensure I'm meeting the needs of my household. It keeps me accountable. It helps me track where I need to be and when. Just because my husband doesn't have a set schedule doesn't mean I can't operate from one that honors the flow of our home. The truth is that I've only started committing to my personal schedule relatively recently. I've finally realized that twenty-four hours is not a lot to share with others when I have a family of four. They are the most important people in my life, and they deserve the best of my time. The Holy Spirit convicted me with this, and I've realized that creating and honoring a personal schedule has made it easier to say 'no' to outside distractions and unnecessary demands. I've come to learn that just because I'm capable doesn't mean I'm available.

So, if your rhythm is already working, honor it. The goal is not uniformity; the goal is unity. Unity can take different forms in each marriage. The key is this: Communicate. Support. Adjust. And always aim for peace.

TACTICAL TIP: Set aside time on a Sunday evening to review the upcoming week as a family. Use this moment to align schedules, clarify responsibilities, and ensure everyone, from husband to children, is on the same page before the week begins.

2. Stewardship of Time & Energy

Time is one of your most sacred resources. If you don't manage it, chaos will. Time is not just a commodity; when we steward it wisely, we protect the atmosphere of our home and the intimacy of our covenant. Ask:

- What drains us most during the week?
- Where do we need margin, not just movement?
- What gets in the way of rest, intimacy, or prayer?

Scripture reminds us "Be very careful, then, how you live, not as unwise but as wise, making the most of every opportunity." (Ephesians 5:15–16, NIV). Wise stewardship of time is obedience. And here's something I've had to learn the hard way. This was once a weak area for me. Honestly, it's one I'm still working on. I used to spend hours in the presence of God. Beautiful, rich time that filled my spirit. But what I didn't realize at first was that I was doing it at the expense of everything else I had been entrusted to steward. I'd get lost in worship, prayer, or Bible study, and by the time I emerged from that space, the rest of the day would be rushed, undone, or stressful. It wasn't that spending time with God was wrong, not at all. But the Holy Spirit lovingly convicted me: "Don't spend time with me on your family's time. Do it on your own time." That might sound strange, but it was a correction that saved my family's rhythm. I was using my husband's time. Time when he wanted to connect with me or relax together, and instead, I was deep in prayer. I was using my children's time, when they needed help, attention, or support and I was trying to fit everything else around the time I spent with God.

God is not going to push you out of His presence. But He will teach you to honor the other assignments He's placed in your hands. So now, I try to reserve my quiet, personal hours for extended worship and study. And I try to keep my husband's time and my children's time clear and sacred, just as I would keep a divine appointment. (Well, my husband has been so gracious in giving me some late nights to finish this book!) Because stewardship is about how you manage all that God has given you. That includes your marriage, your home, your body, and your mind. Your time is like a seed. Steward it well, and it will bear fruit in every area of your life.

TACTICAL TIP: Block out time for connection the way you do for bills or laundry. Protect your time together like a guarded post. Don't let busyness outrank intimacy. Intentionally create moments for laughter, quiet reflection, shared meals, and simple presence.

Sometimes the most sacred space in your week is the one you refuse to overfill.

3. Atmosphere of Peace

We have covered peace quite a lot in previous chapters, but it's so multifaceted. There is no victory without rest, and the truth is, lack of rest is a sure sign of lack of peace. Even in war, soldiers rotate shifts to restore their strength and return to a secure base. Without peace in the atmosphere, even the strongest heart will grow weary. In your home, peace is not just the absence of conflict; it's the presence of God's order, presence, and love. And as a wife, you are often the thermostat of that atmosphere. But what happens when your peace is tested? What happens when your husband forgets to pick up what you asked for from the store? When the car isn't filled up with gas? When a responsibility that was his to carry was left undone? These are real, practical moments that every wife faces. And it's in these very moments that the atmosphere of your home is either sustained or shaken.

Let's be clear: maintaining peace doesn't mean you ignore frustration. It means you choose not to let it govern your response. You remember that your role is not to mirror the chaos, but to command the climate. Peace begins in the secret place. When your soul is anchored, your reactions shift. You become slower to anger, quicker to forgive, and deeply aware that your atmosphere is a spiritual assignment. This is where the grace of adoption comes into play. Just as you've had to adapt before shifting rhythms when your spouse wasn't available or initiating peace when tensions were high, you can continue to do so with wisdom and grace. You can pivot without losing peace. It's about posture, not perfection.

For these moments, I had to learn to surrender, submit and sacrifice. This is not weakness. This is strength under the government of Heaven. Sometimes the real battle isn't the undone task; it's your temptation to let it undo you. The victory is not getting what you want but yielding to who you truly are. Remember, when it's a difficult thing to do, just rename it a sacrifice. Because it's God giving you a moment of surrender on a silver platter.

TACTICAL TIP: Ask God each morning: "What atmosphere do You want me to set today?" Then set practical anchors. Light a candle. Start the day with worship. Diffuse oils. Plan your meals. Have grace with the unexpected. When peace is threatened, reclaim it in prayer. Create a "peace plan" for those recurring moments. Whether it's how you'll respond, retreat, or reset.

Peace is the atmosphere you cultivate, but wisdom is what helps you sustain it. In the next chapter, we'll talk about the allies and advisors who can strengthen your marriage through godly counsel.

Prayer
Father, let Your peace rule my heart and my home. Teach me to govern my tone, my thoughts, and my thresholds. I surrender every urge to control, every need to fix, every fear that rises when things feel out of order. Let me be a place You dwell. Let my home become a sanctuary, even when life feels chaotic. Fill every room with Your presence. In Jesus' name, Amen.

Journal Reflection
What disrupts my peace most often, and how can I address it wisely?

How do I typically respond when others fail to meet expectations?

What does my peace plan look like practically and spiritually?

Do I believe that I carry the authority to command my atmosphere?

FOURTEEN

ALLIES AND ADVISORS SEEKING GODLY COUNSEL

You Were Never Meant to Fight Alone

In every military campaign, victory depends not only on the courage of frontline troops but also on the wisdom, insight, and support from commanders, advisors, and allies behind the scenes. Victory is never achieved in isolation. Yet, many wives fight their battles silently, bearing the burden of emotional strain, spiritual warfare, and relational complexities alone. You were never designed to carry such weight without help. God, in His infinite wisdom and redemptive love, has placed strategic allies and advisors within His Body to walk alongside you, offer clarity, and remind you of His truth when the battle feels overwhelming.

This chapter will equip you to intentionally build a godly support squad. People who sharpen you spiritually, pray earnestly, and remind you who God has called you to be.

Why You Need Counsel and Community

Marriage doesn't require perfection, but it does demand perspective. Emotions can blur vision, and personal pain can cloud discernment. Godly counsel offers:

- *Clarity* in moments of confusion

- *Accountability* when isolation or resentment tempts you

- *Affirmation* of God's promises beyond your current feelings

- *Gentle correction* that protects you from pride, fear, and isolation

Remember, God often communicates His love and Wisdom through the voices of others. Do not silence His voice by isolating yourself.

THREE TYPES OF PEOPLE EVERY WIFE NEEDS

1. You Need a Godly Mentor or Counselor
A mentor or counselor is someone spiritually mature and experienced in navigating marriage and life's complexities. They listen intently, challenge graciously, and guide lovingly:

- They seek God's heart, not just your comfort

- They help you process your emotions through the lens of truth, rather than merely venting frustrations

- They gently encourage growth rather than allowing you to remain stuck

Biblical Example:
Consider Naomi's mentorship of Ruth (Ruth 3). Ruth found herself in a vulnerable place: widowed, alone, and uncertain about her future. Yet, Naomi's seasoned wisdom and loving guidance helped position Ruth strategically for her destiny. Through Naomi's insightful instructions and prayerful support, Ruth's life

transformed from one of grief to a powerful testimony of redemption. Her obedience to wise counsel ultimately led her into Boaz's care, becoming part of Christ's lineage. God's redemptive love beautifully unfolded through the trusted voice of Naomi.

2. You Need a Spiritual Sister or Prayer Partner

A prayer partner walks with you spiritually and practically. This is someone who understands your struggles firsthand, offering support through prayer and mutual encouragement:

- They provide emotional solidarity, reminding you that you are not alone

- They commit to intercession, lifting your concerns faithfully before God

There's a misconception that married women should only seek advice from other married women, but that simply isn't true. Single friends and family members can offer powerful, Spirit-led wisdom and life-giving perspective. You don't have to be married to hear from God about marriage. Single women have counseled and prayed me back to strength during low seasons. At the same time, married sisters also bring deep understanding through shared experience. Both voices are valuable. Don't limit who God may use.

Biblical Example:

Consider the story of Mary and Elizabeth (Luke 1:39–45). Here were two women facing deeply extraordinary and potentially isolating circumstances. Elizabeth was advanced in age, carrying the forerunner of Christ, and Mary, a young woman facing a miraculous yet socially challenging pregnancy. Elizabeth's husband, Zechariah, was unable to speak, which likely intensified her feelings of isolation. Meanwhile, Mary was navigating circumstances that could have easily led to misunderstanding and loneliness. Yet, God strategically orchestrated their meeting. The angel specifically directed Mary toward Elizabeth, providing her with a clear path to support and encouragement. When Mary entered Elizabeth's home, Elizabeth's child leapt joyfully in her womb, and Elizabeth was filled with the Holy Spirit, immediately recognizing and affirming Mary's divine calling. In that sacred moment, Mary found not only emotional comfort but also prophetic confirmation of her purpose.

Elizabeth provided Mary with a safe place to rest and be strengthened, welcoming her warmly for three months during a crucial period in her pregnancy. This powerful encounter illustrates an important truth: God intentionally places people in your path who will affirm your identity, confirm His promises, and provide the strength and companionship you need to fulfill your calling. Just as He led Mary to Elizabeth, trust that God will guide you to the allies and advisors you need for your marriage.

3. You Need a Professional Counselor
Seeking professional counseling or therapy is not a sign of weak faith; it is faith activated:

- Seek the help of a professional if unresolved issues keep resurfacing.

- Seek immediate counsel if emotional abuse, manipulation, or trauma is involved.

I understand that clinical counselors are not always available to everyone due to limitations beyond their control. However, I encourage you to take advantage of the free government or community services that are available. Don't be embarrassed. Your marriage is worth fighting for, and seeking help is wisdom. Also, don't pressure your husband to go to counseling with you if he's not ready. Instead, pray and trust God to move on his heart at the right time.

I remember a season when I deeply desired for my husband to attend counseling with me. He wasn't interested, and I felt discouraged. But then, I came across a short video clip from a couple I admire. In that moment, I was reminded of a powerful truth: I didn't need to fix my husband; I could begin by allowing God to work on me. So, I went to counseling alone. And I can honestly say that it transformed our marriage because it transformed me.

Professional counselors, equipped with both clinical knowledge and faith-based spiritual insight, can provide tools and healing pathways that go beyond what friends or mentors may offer. This is not about replacing prayer; it's about pairing prayer with the specialized training and therapeutic tools that only a professional counselor may be able to provide.

Biblical Wisdom: "Where there is no guidance, a people falls, but in an abundance of counselors there is safety." (Proverbs 11:14, ESV)

Who Not to Seek Advice From
Be discerning, and avoid:

- Voices that validate your emotions without encouraging spiritual maturity. While empathy is valuable, growth requires truth and accountability.

- People who harbor bitterness or unresolved pain related to marriage or men. This can taint their perspective.

- Those who offer advice but show no effort toward healthy fruit in their own relationships. While even a struggling person may share truth, look for counsel that is not only spoken but also lived.

- Carnal viewpoints that exclude God's Spirit and truth. Even the most well-meaning advice can mislead if not rooted in God's Word and love.

You want voices that are biblically rooted, humble, and honest. These are the voices that guide you in truth and mercy. The voices that carry the heart of God. Remember, you are seen and deeply loved by God. His plan for you includes supportive relationships that build you up, guide your steps, and remind you of His steadfast love. Lean into community. Embrace counsel. Your victory is not just possible, it is available in Christ.

God is faithful in providing godly voices to guide you, however, there are moments when only your faith will hold you. In the next chapter, we'll discuss the will to stand and how to develop resilient faith that remains strong under pressure.

Prayer

Father, thank You that I don't have to fight alone. Send the right voices into my life; mentors, friends, and counselors who carry Your wisdom and heart. Help me receive truth with humility and let go of voices that distract or harm. Teach me to discern who's meant to walk with me in this season. In Jesus' name, Amen.

Journal Reflection

Do I have spiritually grounded, wise counselors and friends in my circle?

Have I rejected godly advice simply because it made me uncomfortable?

What kind of voice or mentor does my marriage need in this season?

Field Drill: Support Squad Assessment

This week, take inventory:

- Who currently speaks into your life and marriage?

- Who should you invite closer or open up to?

- Who might God be prompting you to distance yourself from?

Write their names. Pray over them. Ask God to help you release them.

FIFTEEN

THE WILL TO WITHSTAND CULTIVATING RESILIENT FAITH

When the War Wears on

In military endurance training, soldiers are taught not only to fight, but also to endure. They are trained to survive harsh conditions, endure long marches, carry heavy loads, and remain alert even when sleep-deprived or emotionally spent. It is not just the strength of their weapons that determines their success, but the strength of their will. Marriage also calls for this kind of resilience. Sometimes, the war you're facing in your home or heart will feel long. And in those moments, it won't be the flashiness of faith that carries you; it will be the grit of it. The quiet, stubborn resolve that says, "I will trust God anyway."

This chapter is about building that kind of faith. A resilient, rooted, Spirit-empowered faith that doesn't collapse under pressure. By now, if you've been walking through this book from Chapter One, you should already have a vision, a mission, and a mandate for your marriage. That clarity alone becomes a weapon. Because when you know what you're fighting for, you won't quit easily. You are not fighting aimlessly; you're fighting with purpose. And that purpose gives your endurance power.

Why Resilient Faith Matters in Marriage

Resilient faith is not about denying pain or pretending everything is fine. It is about enduring with perspective. It gives you the ability to remain steadfast when prayers take time to be answered, stay spiritually engaged even when emotionally drained, believe God's promises in the face of present contradictions, and continue building when you feel like giving up. There will be seasons that test your spiritual stamina, and faith will be your fuel.

WHAT RESILIENCE LOOKS LIKE

1. Holding on When You Want to Give Up

Faith is tested most when your emotions and circumstances tell you to quit. But Hebrews 10:36 reminds us: "You need to persevere so that when you have done the will of God, you will receive what he has promised." (Hebrews 10:36, NIV).

2. Choosing Obedience Over Emotion

Feelings change. God's Word does not. Obedience in hard seasons is one of the greatest expressions of faith. It says, "God, I don't feel like it today, but I'm going to love, serve, forgive, and pray anyway." I spoke about this two times already in earlier chapters. When obedience feels hard, I see it as God handing me a moment of sacrifice on a silver platter. And there is no sacrifice, when done right, that God does not honor. He will meet you right in that place of obedience and sacrifice. When you push past feelings and press into faith, you invite the power of Heaven into your circumstance.

3. Speaking Life into Dead Places

Faith doesn't just endure, it declares. Like Ezekiel in the valley of dry bones, you are called to prophesy life over what looks dead. Speak God's Word over your marriage. Faith is vocal. Let's look at it this way: How do you know something looks dead or barren? Because you know what the opposite of that looks like. Jesus died and resurrected so you could have access to the opposite of what looks lifeless. Speak life and fruitfulness no matter what. That is your truth. That is your ending. Like Ezekiel, prophesy the entire outcome of what your life should look like, not just that it will live, but that it will thrive based on the vision God gave you.

4. Remembering Your Testimonies

Never underestimate the power of your past victories. Remind yourself what God has already done. David said, "The Lord who delivered me from the paw of the lion and the paw of the bear will deliver me from the hand of this Philistine." (1 Samuel 17:37, NIV). Let your history with God fuel your hope. This is what I love about faith; it's built on history. You have history with God. Pull on those receipts. Remind yourself how He came through before. The same God who provided, healed, restored, or rescued in the past is still faithful today. Your faith isn't rooted in outcomes or declarations. Your faith is rooted in a God who is able to do exceedingly and abundantly above all you could ever ask or think (Ephesians 3:20). That history with God isn't just a memory; it's a weapon. Use it.

Spiritual Endurance is Built, not Borrowed

You can't borrow someone else's endurance. You must build your own. This doesn't mean striving in your own strength. It means leaning into grace, abiding in God's Word, and allowing trials to produce spiritual maturity (James 1:2–4). Like muscles trained under weight, your spirit strengthens under pressure. Your suffering is not in vain. When you come out of this, issues like this won't be able to stand before you, not another day in your life. God is allowing it, not just to build your endurance and fortify your faith in Him but hear this: 'The Egyptians whom you see today, you shall never see again.' (Exodus 14:13, ESV). Trust the God of your process. You will get to the other side. Don't give up.

Refined in the Waiting: Jesus, My First Husband

One thing that has anchored me in seasons when things didn't look how I desired them to in my marriage is this: I already have a perfect Husband in Heaven. Isaiah 54:5 reminds us, 'For your Maker is your husband, the Lord of hosts is his name.'' (Isaiah 54:5, ESV). This means I am never without covering, never without covenant. Even when things in my marriage feel out of sync, I can lean on the one who is always consistent, Christ, my Bridegroom.

This section is not just for wives, but also for wives in waiting. When you truly understand that Jesus is your first Bridegroom, your heart begins to shift. Instead of placing pressure on a man to be all things, you begin to see your situation differently. You begin to ask, "Lord, what are You working out in me through this?" Again, God won't always change the circumstance immediately, because He's trying to change you. There are moments in your union when it's not about the other person. It's not even about the situation. It's about you being transformed. It's about the Spirit of God using what feels hard, to mature you, stretch you, and increase your capacity. Because what good is it if the external situation shifts but your internal strength remains small? What good is a restored marriage if you're still living with the same wounded mindset, the same emotional fragility, the same spiritual immaturity that can't carry the blessing?

God isn't just interested in giving you what you ask for. He wants to form the kind of woman who can maintain what He gives. He wants to enlarge your heart, sharpen your discernment, and root you so deeply in Him that, whether your husband is walking in complete alignment or not, you remain steady. That's the power of covenant with Christ. You are not alone in this. You're not just submitting to your husband; you're submitting to God's process. And the truth is: He is a faithful Husband. He sees every tear. He responds to every act of obedience. And as He perfects what concerns you. He is perfecting you. So don't resist the refining. Let this process make you stronger, softer, wiser, and more like Him. He knows exactly how to finish what He started.

ENDURANCE IN THE EVERYDAY STORIES OF BIBLE WOMEN

Spiritual endurance often looks like obedience in places that feel unchanging. It's not just about persevering in crisis. It's about showing up with faith in the mundane. Throughout Scripture, God consistently honors women who remained rooted where He placed them, even when life didn't feel prophetic or purposeful. Let's discuss a few of them.

The Woman at the Well (John 4:1–42)

She wasn't fasting. She wasn't on a spiritual retreat. She was just showing up at the same place she always had, carrying the same jar, hoping for water that never fully satisfied. She had lived through five broken relationships and was now with a man who wasn't even her husband. And still, Jesus walked across town, sat at the well, and waited for her. He waited, not just as Savior, but as the Bridegroom. He didn't ask for performance. He asked for truth. And when she answered, "I have no husband," she was speaking beyond her relationship status. She was speaking to the ache of someone who had never truly been found by a man willing to be a husband in covenant. And yet, here was the seventh man. Her number of completion. The man who would not just know her story but rewrite it. He revealed Himself plainly: "I who speak to you am He." She didn't go looking for Him, but in her faithfulness to the routine, He found her.

Hannah (1 Samuel 1:1–28; 2:1–11)

Hannah, the barren woman who poured out her soul before the Lord. She showed up in her anguish year after year. She kept praying, kept weeping, kept believing even when it looked foolish. She was ridiculed by her rival and misunderstood by the priest, yet she stayed in posture. She never stopped coming. And in her enduring prayer, God didn't just give her a child; He gave her a prophet. Samuel wasn't just her breakthrough; he was God's answer for a generation. And He found her faithful in her anguish.

Ruth (Ruth 1–4)

She gleaned in the fields. Not to be seen, but to survive. She wasn't strategizing for a husband or manipulating the system. She was honoring her commitment to Naomi, waking up each morning to fulfill her obligations. And Boaz noticed not just her beauty, but her faithfulness as well. He told her, "All that you have done... has been fully told to me." Her story of resilience preceded her. She didn't chase favor. Favor found her working in the ordinary.

Rebekah at the Well (Genesis 24:10–27)

She was going to the well to draw water just as she likely had many times before. There was no announcement that her life was about to change. No angelic visitation. Just a servant on assignment, praying for a sign. And in her willingness to serve, to draw water for both man and his camels, she stepped into divine selection. She became the wife of Isaac and part of a covenant lineage. All because she was faithfully positioned at the well.

Anna (Luke 2:36–38)

Anna was a prophetess, advanced in years, who had lived with her husband for only seven years before becoming a widow. For eighty-four years she remained in the temple, worshiping, fasting, and praying. She wasn't chasing visibility or hoping for applause. She simply stayed faithful where God had placed her. And when Jesus was brought into the temple as an infant, Anna recognized Him. The Messiah entered the very place where she had been waiting. Her reward met her in the posture of consistency.

What makes Anna's story even more powerful is that she didn't just pray for the coming Messiah. She saw Him. She saw the Deliverer of Israel with her own eyes. She saw her true Bridegroom, the Christ, even if He appeared as a child in that moment. For every widow, this is a prophetic sign of hope: that even in widowhood, God is able to reveal Himself as the Husband who never dies. Anna's life declares that you don't have to leave this earth before seeing your Bridegroom again. In the place of loss, He shows up as the One who restores hope and fulfills every promise.

This is also a reminder: it is okay to desire marriage again. Why? Because your ultimate Bridegroom still lives. "For your Maker is your husband— the Lord Almighty is his name— the Holy One of Israel is your Redeemer; He is called the God of all the earth" (Isaiah 54:5, NIV). The One who can never die continues to fulfill desires, even as He secures your heart in Himself. To long for earthly companionship does not cancel out your covenant with Him. It flows from knowing that the true Bridegroom is alive, present, and faithful.

Don't Move. Stay Faithful.

These women weren't striving for breakthrough. They were living in their assignments. They were faithful in the roles they held, daughter, servant, intercessor, mother-in-waiting, wife-in-waiting positions. And that faithfulness became the soil where God planted the next move of their lives. Resilient faith is not always loud. Sometimes it's quiet obedience. It's staying where God placed you when the results don't come fast. It's trusting that if you're where He assigned you to be, He will send what belongs to you. And that's what the enemy fears most. He knows he can't touch your promise, so he tries to get you to move out of position, because he knows that what Heaven has for you will meet you in your obedience, not in your striving, but in your staying.

Don't despise your routine. Don't abandon your role. Keep drawing from the well. Keep showing up to the temple. Keep gleaning in the field. Keep praying even when it feels empty. Because what God has spoken will not miss you. And what's for you doesn't require striving; it only requires you to remain. Remaining keeps you aligned. In the next chapter, we'll explore post-war reconciliation and the healing that makes wholeness possible.

Prayer

Father, some days feel long, and the weight of it all feels too much. But I know You are faithful. Strengthen my faith not just for the outcome, but for the process. Help me to trust You in the waiting and to obey even when it's hard. Teach me to endure like Hannah, to prophesy like Ezekiel, and to believe like David. Jesus, You are my first Husband. Help me to rest in Your perfection when I feel disappointed by what I see. Refine me in this waiting. Increase my capacity, transform my character, and build a woman who can carry Your glory in her home. I surrender again today. Use even this season for Your glory. In Jesus' name, Amen.

Journal Reflection
Where am I tempted to give up, and have I forgotten the vision, mission, and mandate God gave me for this marriage?

What has God already done for me that I need to remember and draw strength from?

Am I obeying even when I don't feel like it, treating these moments as divine opportunities for sacrifice and alignment?

How am I fueling my faith daily so that I can declare life even when things feel barren?

Am I letting this waiting season refine me, or am I just waiting for the situation to change?

Do I believe that Jesus is my faithful Husband, and am I allowing Him to shape me in this process?

Tactical Drill: Fortify Your Faith
Choose one spiritual discipline to focus on daily this week:

- Pray in the Spirit
- Meditate on Scripture
- Fast
- Speak declarations out loud
- Journal answered prayers

SIXTEEN

POST-WAR RECONCILIATION & HEALING

After the Battle Ends

Every war leaves wounds, but God never leaves you in them. His heart is always for healing, restoration, and redemption. In marriage, conflict may end, but that doesn't mean healing has happened. Just because peace has returned to the home doesn't mean reconnection has returned to the heart. This chapter is about what happens after the war: the sacred work of reconciliation, rebuilding trust, and walking in emotional and spiritual healing. Because God doesn't just want your marriage to stop fighting. He wants it to start thriving.

The Myth of "Moving on"

Time alone doesn't heal wounds. It simply buries them deeper if they're never addressed. Real healing requires:

- Honest conversation
- Confession and repentance
- Listening without defense
- Choosing grace over grudges
- Rebuilding, not just resuming

If you skip the healing process, you will likely repeat the same conflict patterns. Healing is not optional; it is the path to peace. And it's never just emotional; it is spiritual. It is warfare against bitterness, distance, and numbness. Healing is not for the faint of heart, but for those who dare to believe in restoration. If this is you, there are signs that reveal when wounds are still unhealed:

- You shut down or "numb out" emotionally
- You replay arguments in your mind
- You avoid intimacy or connection
- You've apologized, but still feel resentful
- You've forgiven, but not fully released the pain

If you recognize yourself here, you are not broken; you are human. And here is the good news: your wounds don't disqualify you; they are the very places God desires to touch with His restoring power. Below, I will explore three paths to post-war healing.

THREE PATHS TO POST-WAR HEALING

Path One: Heart-Level Honesty

Healing begins with truth, not blame. And it often starts with the courage to slow down and ask God to reveal what is really happening beneath the surface. Ask yourself:

- What truly hurt me, not just the words or actions, but what it triggered inside of me?

- What did I need in that moment that I never expressed?

- What beliefs have I carried about myself or my spouse that may not even be true?

Bring those questions to God before you bring them to your spouse. Let Him sift your emotions through grace and truth. Many times, our first reaction in marriage does not reflect what we actually need, it reflects unspoken expectations or unhealed places.

I remember a night when I reacted negatively to something that was not even my husband's fault. Instead of staying in the room, I told him I needed to step away and process with God. I ended up falling asleep on the couch, and by morning I had never returned to bed.

Now, that is not something we do. We do not sleep apart. So, when he woke up and realized I was not there, it really bothered him. And honestly, part of me was defensive. I said, "Well, if it bothered you so much, why didn't you come get me? Why didn't you check on me?" Because deep down, what I really wanted was for him to pacify my wound. It was like I had a boo-boo, and I wanted him to kiss it and make it better.

But the truth is, he had fallen asleep because he was in the bed where he was supposed to be. And when we finally talked about it, the first thing he did was remind me of something I had said earlier that very day. I had been reflecting on a wife who suddenly lost her husband and the father of her children. I told him how painful it must be to go to bed alone, how I never wanted to experience that kind of emptiness. I even said to him, "Our bed feels cold when you're not in it," and I prayed out loud for mercy.

He looked at me and said, "I heard you. I heard your prayer. But then you left your safe place, the very bed you said you never wanted to feel empty and cold, because of a wound I was not even responsible for."

And then, after holding me accountable, he gave me the words I did not even know I needed. He did not give me the comfort speech I was expecting. Instead, he said, "You are my favorite place to be. You give me rest. I look forward to being in the presence of my wife. I do not ever want to be apart from you. When I leave work, I am filled with joy because I get to come home to you."

At first, I thought, "You are making this about you. You are not even addressing my wound. You are minimizing what I am feeling. This is not what I need right now." But God showed me it was exactly what my soul needed. My husband was not ignoring my wound, he was pulling me higher. He was taking me to a place where I could see that my wound and affliction was nothing compared to what was happening for me now.

That is what heart-level honesty looks like: being willing to recognize the difference between what feels good in the moment and what actually heals.

Path Two: Grace-Filled Reconciliation

Reconciliation is not pretending everything is fine just to avoid more conflict. It is the holy work of humility, choosing peace over pride, ownership over defense, and forgiveness over distance.

That night taught me that reconciliation does not always look like pacifying each other's wounds. Sometimes it looks like being lovingly confronted and then invited into a higher perspective. My husband did not minimize me, he reminded me of what I had already declared. He called me back to my safe place. And then he covered me with words that rebuilt my confidence in who I was to him.

And here is the mystery of reconciliation: when you resolve conflict God's way, you do not just go back to normal, you grow through it. Our intimacy after that moment was not just restored, it was transformed. I found myself blushing at the mall, looking at my husband like I was falling in love all over again. In church, during prayer, I could not even keep my focus because my heart was giggling like a schoolgirl just watching him. I had to close my eyes and regroup myself. That is what reconciliation does, it takes what once felt like a breaking point and turns it into a deeper bond.

Psalm 84 says, "Better is one day in Your courts than a thousand elsewhere." The psalmist was expressing how nothing compares to simply being in God's presence. And in that moment, I realized my husband was saying the very same thing about me. Even in the middle of conflict, he did not want me to pull away. He still wanted me close. He was reminding me that what mattered most to him was not that everything felt perfect, but that my presence remained intact.

And that revelation drew me deeper into Christ as well. Because reconciliation in marriage is designed to mirror reconciliation with Him. Christ does not ignore our wounds, but neither does He let them create distance. He's saying, "I do not care what you think disqualifies you. I do not care how broken you feel. I have wounds too. In fact, I bore them for you. Just do not pull away from Me. Do not put distance between us."

That is what reconciliation looks like. It closes the gap. It restores presence. It deepens intimacy. And it leaves both husband and wife stronger than before, just as it leaves us stronger in Christ.

Path Three: Spiritual and Emotional Repair

Some wounds go deeper than a single conversation can reach. Reconciliation may close the distance in the moment, but lasting healing often requires consistent pursuit, spiritually, emotionally, and even practically. This is where spiritual repair must be activated:

- Intercession: Praying with and for one another, inviting God to mend places you cannot reach.

- Fasting: Setting aside time to seek clarity, intimacy, or breakthrough together.

- Counseling or Inner Healing: Allowing trusted leaders or trained professionals to help you uncover hidden roots and apply godly wisdom.

- Time with Intentional Pursuit: Choosing daily acts of kindness, presence, and affection that water the soil of your covenant.

Healing is both restoration and process. God will do the miraculous work, but He invites you to participate in it. Sometimes the first step is as simple as praying together even when it feels uncomfortable. Other times, it is seeking help outside of your marriage, because wholeness is too valuable to leave to chance.

And if your spouse is not ready to walk that path yet, do not force it. Begin with God. Your personal healing can become the very doorway to your marital restoration. Conflict handled God's way has the power to deepen intimacy, but sustained repair keeps that intimacy flourishing.

Do not normalize dysfunction. Normalize healing and wholeness. Do what you must to get to that place. Because your marriage is worth it. And you are worth it.

Biblical Example: Peter and Jesus — Restoration After Denial

Peter had failed Jesus publicly and repeatedly. And even after the resurrection, something still lingered between them. But Jesus didn't ignore the fracture. He initiated a private, gentle moment on the shore (John 21). "Do you love Me?" He asked. Not to condemn, but to reaffirm. To heal. To recommission. That's what Jesus does. He meets us in the silence. In the shame. In the distance. And then He restores, with both love and assignment. That's the kind of healing He offers your marriage, too.

God specializes in resurrection. What feels lifeless can live again. What feels too wounded can be restored. You may not know how to rebuild, but your Healer does. So don't fake peace. Don't skip over the ache. Do the work with Him. Because your marriage doesn't just need calm, it needs wholeness. Healing doesn't happen in the shadows. Let God bring light to what still needs mending. Let Him love you back into wholeness.

A healed and whole marriage doesn't just bless you and your spouse; it shapes the atmosphere in which your children grow up. In the next chapter, we'll talk about how to raise sons and daughters who are warriors for the Kingdom.

Prayer

Father, I invite You into the broken places. Into the words I can't forget and the wounds I haven't named. Heal the places where I've shut down, hardened, or become numb. Create in me a pure heart, O God, one that sees rightly, feels deeply, and responds tenderly. Teach me to forgive with Your strength. Help me to speak truth with grace. Where there has been destruction, plant restoration. Where there has been fear, awaken love. In Jesus' name, Amen.

Journal Reflection

What unresolved conflict, memory, or unprocessed experience might still be influencing how I show up in my marriage?

Have I truly brought this to God, or have I buried it, hoping time would erase the pain?

What is one small step of healing, prayer, counseling, confession, or forgiveness that I sense God is asking me to take today?

Have I invited God to purify my heart so I can see clearly again my spouse, myself, and His hand at work?

Field Drill: Rebuilding

Choose one of the following to practice this week:

- Write a letter of grace to your husband — speak from your healed place, thanking him for the love, peace, and partnership that God is restoring between you. Write it as though it already is

- Say, "I forgive you," or "I'm sorry," out loud. Not because it's easy, but because it's holy

SEVENTEEN

RAISING WARRIOR MARRIAGE AS MINISTRY

Your Home is a Forward Operating Base

In every war, the frontlines matter, but so does the base. The military doesn't just win battles out in the field. Victory is shaped at the base, where soldiers are trained, equipped, fed, and deployed. That's your home. It is a forward operating base for the Kingdom. What happens behind the walls, what's said, what's modeled, and what's cultivated is where the next generation of soldiers are formed. This chapter isn't just about parenting; it's about preparation and Kingdom legacy. The home is both a battleground and a boot camp, where warriors are not only protected but made. Because those you train within your walls will one day walk out and face the world. And when they do, they don't just fight their own battles; they carry forward the mission of your house.

Your children are the torchbearers of your legacy. They are watching you, studying you, and becoming what you model. In training them, you are not just raising children; you are also shaping their future. You are shaping the future of the world. One day, they will pick up the baton where you left off and advance the Kingdom further than you ever could alone.

A Personal Story: Why This Matters

My husband and I have two children, but three pregnancies. Each one has shaped the way I see parenting and deepened my understanding of God's purpose for family. We had our first daughter, Nala a year after we got married. At that time, we were not yet saved. We weren't thinking about her destiny or what she would one day do for God. We just wanted to start a family. But even in our limited understanding, she was the joy of our lives. We couldn't wait to meet her.

Our second child, Micah came unexpectedly. He broke through every barrier of contraception. God allowed him to enter the world in His own timing. By then, we were saved, but we weren't planning for another child yet. Still, he came, and we cannot imagine a world without him. He is one of the most amazing little boys you will ever know.

Our third pregnancy was different. By then, we had a revelation of what it truly means to have children, not just for ourselves, but for the Kingdom. We prayed for her. We named her Zoe before we even conceived her, as a declaration of the life of Christ. We prayed so specifically that we said, "God, if this child will not live for You, don't even allow us to conceive." And yet, we did conceive her. But at 33 weeks, her heart stopped beating. That loss devastated me.

It was especially difficult because I had already seen God's mercy at work with my other two children. At Nala's birth, her heart rate kept dropping so low during labor that the doctors were preparing to take her out immediately. And even after she was born, a hospital error led to her being given the wrong shot, which caused her tiny heart to race abnormally fast. She had to be kept on a heart monitor for 24 hours, but God, in His mercy, kept her.

With my son, both his heart rate and mine dropped dangerously low at the same time, and the doctors had to use a vacuum to deliver him quickly. On top of that, he was born with blood type incompatibility that made him unwell and required him to be treated in the NICU until he was strong enough to come home. But again, God's hand was with us. He saved him, and He saved me.

But this time, with Zoe, He did not intervene the way I expected. I wrestled. I questioned God: "Lord, I don't understand. We prayed. We were intentional. We wanted this child for You. Why?"

It was in that grief that God spoke. He said:

"I'm going to do you one better. You will still multiply life. You will multiply yourself by multiplying what Zoe represented. Not only will you raise your own children, but through your life, and your obedience, you will raise children across the world to love Me, to fear Me, and to walk in My ways. As you multiply yourself as a wife, as a mother, and as My daughter, you will transform homes and rescue families across the world."

That was the seed of this book. This book marks the beginning of my journey to multiply myself as a wife. Please forgive me in advance for the length of this chapter, because this chapter is the beginning of me multiplying myself as a mother.

This is where so many parents miss it. We all don't understand why God allows us to become parents, but without that understanding, we can mishandle the privilege. But when you realize that your children are not just yours, they are arrows in the hand of God, part of His redemptive plan for humanity, you will operate differently, and parenting stops being about survival or status, and becomes about stewardship.

Training Loved Warriors

Before our children are called to war, they must be empowered by your love. They must be deeply loved. Not for what they do, how they behave, or how well they perform, but for who they are. This is the first equipping. And it is our first assignment as parents. The Bible teaches children to honor their father and mother, and many parents cling to that command; rightly so. "Honour thy father and thy mother: that thy days may be long upon the land which the Lord thy God giveth thee" (Exodus 20:12, KJV). Paul echoed it when he wrote, "Honor your father and mother"—which is the first commandment with a promise— (Ephesians 6:2, NIV). But what the Lord showed me is this: before a child can learn honor, they must first be loved.

Honor is not the seed; it is the fruit. Just as we, the children of God, grow in honor through receiving the Father's love, so our children will grow in honor when they feel safe, seen, and nurtured. Our children honoring us should not be our first goal. Our first goal should be to love them. Their honor will be taught. It will be learned. But love must be known through experience. It is love that draws us to repentance. It is love that compels us to worship. And it is love, not duty, that causes a child to grow up knowing how to honor both their earthly and heavenly Father.

We can't assume our love is being experienced just because we're meeting basic obligation. It's quite easy to meet certain requirements but totally miss relationship. You can be very busy covering their needs, but not touching their hearts. Yes, we provide. Yes, we correct. Yes, we teach. But affection, presence, tone, and attention, these are the language of love a child understands. Our babies need more than provision. They need presence.

When I lost Zoe, I never got to hold her alive outside the womb. I never got to hear her cry or kiss her cheeks. I never got to love on her the way I wanted to. I grieved that loss deeply. Not just her life, but the expressions of love I never got to give. And in my grief, I became a child again. I held onto God with everything in me. In the place of brokenness, I learned how to receive my Father's love again. That moment was more than pain. It was preparation. God was showing me what it means to be fully dependent, fully surrendered, fully loved. And that revelation is even changing how I mother my children now. They, too, are weak and vulnerable at times. They, too, don't always know what's best for them. But one thing they will never forget is whether they felt loved. And yes, we know love is more than a feeling—but intentionally meeting a child where they are, through expressions of love they understand, becomes a powerful weapon against rejection both now and in the future. When children feel accepted and wanted by you as their mother, it lays a clear pathway for them to grasp the eternal acceptance of God:

> "The Spirit you received does not make you slaves, so that you live in fear again; rather, the Spirit you received brought about your adoption to sonship. And by him we cry, 'Abba, Father.' The Spirit himself testifies with our spirit that we are God's children. Now if we are children, then we are heirs—heirs of God and co-heirs with Christ" (Romans 8:15–17, NIV).

Even as a little girl, I remember how impactful feeling wanted was. My parents separated when I was six years old, and my younger, but older sister and I went to live with our grandmother. Though we were provided for, what I missed most was affection. I was still a child who needed to be held, kissed, and snuggled. And while my grandmother loved me the best way she knew how, I held onto the warmth of my mother's voice on the phone. I lived off the sweetness of her tone. Her simple "my baby" carried me through years of separation.

My mother would visit when she could. I remember finding one of her bras at my grandmother's house, left behind after a visit, and I would sleep with it every night because it smelled like her. Her scent, her sweetness, her presence meant everything to me. When she did visit, I lit up. Her presence alone healed something in me. And when I eventually went back to live with her at ten years old, it was like no time had been lost. She wrapped me in love and affection like only a mother can. She picked up right where she left off, and I didn't need gifts or explanations; I just needed her.

My father struggled with alcoholism for most of my childhood. He passed away when I was ten years old. Many of my memories of him are clouded by the times he was drunk, but the few moments I remember him sober, those are the ones that have stayed with me. Those rare, clear moments shine brighter than all the rest. I was the baby of the family, and maybe that had something to do with how love came to me. I was covered, hugged, kissed, and protected. I knew what it meant to be adored. Though my father's life was cut short, the way he made me feel when he was alive and sober lives on inside me. At thirty-eight years old, I can still feel the warmth of those moments. I can still remember how his presence, when clear and intentional, made me feel like the most loved little girl in the world.

There was one moment in particular I'll never forget. I missed him so much while living with my grandmother that I wrote him a letter, just a little girl with a big heart, longing for her father. And somehow, he received it. There was no phone where he lived, but he found a call box and reached out to me. I still remember the sound of his voice, how it lit something up inside me. I had told him I thought I might need glasses, that I couldn't see well at school, and he was so concerned. I could hear the love in his tone.

That call, that moment, made me feel like I was the happiest child alive. It was a deposit of love that stayed with me long after he was gone.

Even my siblings helped fill in the gaps. When my sister and I would go home on holidays or they would visit us, we felt like we belonged. They hugged us with excitement and made us feel treasured. It didn't matter how long we had been apart. Their affection reminded us that we were seen and loved, and this space was truly our home.

Looking back, I realize those moments were more than memories; they were training. Every time I was held, kissed, called "my baby," or made to feel wanted, my heart was being prepared to recognize the love of my Heavenly Father. God was teaching me, even as a child, what love feels like so I would not mistake its counterfeit later in life. Because I knew love in such pure form, I grew up able to discern what love is and what it is not. That training shaped my decisions as an adult. It anchored me. Even in seasons where circumstances were far from perfect, the love I had received became the standard that pointed me back to God.

God used those moments to prepare me to receive His love. They softened my heart and shaped my theology, not through sermons or doctrine, but through love and affection. Without understanding the depth of it, I experienced God first through the way I was loved by my remarkable family: my parents, Reginald Gordon, and Joan Jonson-Bartley, and my siblings, Andrae Morris, Orville Gordon, Rowland Gordon, Marsha Gordon, Pauline Grant, Julia Gordon, and Jewel Gordon.

I can see now that even through the brokenness, My Father in Heaven was always with me. This is why I believe so deeply that love is not optional for a child. It's not a luxury; it's a lifeline, like oxygen. Every moment of real love, even in imperfect families, is a prophetic seed. Those moments will train a child to know how to receive from God one day. If we want to raise children who know how to worship, how to trust, how to hear God's voice, we must first raise children who know they are loved, so they will know how to receive the love of God, and never doubt Him as their Father. This is what we give our children when we love them well: the ability to trust God.

Children Don't Always Remember the Lack—They Remember the Love

Sometimes I hear my siblings share memories of struggle from our childhood, stories of the lights being disconnected, or of meals being scarce, or moments when our parents were doing their best with very little. And I believe them. I know those days were real. But here's what's amazing: I barely remember the lack. And it's not because I wasn't there, but because I was a child. Children don't always register the burden their parents carry. They don't count how many slices of bread are left or wonder if this dinner might be the last meal of the day. They're not thinking about whether the clothes they wear came from a sacrifice. All they know is what they feel. And when they feel loved, it becomes their anchor memory.

Even now, looking back, I know I lived through some of those seasons. But when I close my eyes and think about my childhood, what stands out are not on the moments of need, but the moments of love. Moments where I felt cherished. Seen. Covered. Held. Yes, I have some painful memories, but in His mercy, God has made the good memories greater. The ones filled with warmth. The ones where I was being picked up and twirled around. The ones where I smelled my mother's perfume on a shirt she left behind and hugged it close like it was her arms. The ones where my father, even though a struggling life, still made me feel like his baby girl when he was sober. The ones where my brothers stepped in to love and shield me when my father was no longer

184

alive to do so. The ones where my sisters made me feel covered, seen, and guided. This is the power of being loved well as a child: you're shielded, even in seasons of lack.

Some of us are still caught up in who was supposed to love us, and we must be careful not to pass that on to our children. They should learn that the Father's love may come through different vessels, but it always comes. If we're not healed in our own hearts, we'll miss the many ways God is showing up. We'll withhold the very lesson we were meant to model: that love may not be found in who gave birth to you, but it's in who showed up. We need to heal from the expectation that love has to look a certain way or come from a specific person. Otherwise, we'll raise our children to chase a version of love that was never real, instead of recognizing and receiving the love that God has faithfully provided. If we can't recognize love for ourselves, we won't be able to reflect it to our children. Let the healing begin with you, so it can flow to them.

To the One Who Grew up Too Fast

As a woman, I want to speak to every mother reading this. Every wife. Every daughter who grew up too fast. You're still someone's child. You may feel like you are carrying the weight of the world or bear the burden of your household on your shoulders, but I invite you to become small again in God's presence. To let the Father love you. To remember not just what broke you, but what held you, and is still holding you now.

Sometimes we spend so much time replaying what went wrong, we forget the sacred beauty of what went right. You may have grown up in a house full of dysfunction, but did anyone hug you? Did someone call your name with tenderness? Did someone ever make you feel safe, even for a moment? If so, don't dismiss it. Don't call it small and overlook it. Those were God's fingerprints. They were Heaven's rescue missions wrapped in hugs, braids, hand-me-downs, and hot meals. And maybe they were few and far between. But they were real. And they were powerful. And they kept you. You made it here. Not because everything went right, but because God made sure you received love somewhere, somehow, through someone. And now that you're a parent, you get to make sure your children don't grow up bound, but to do that, you must be free first. You must be willing to embrace your own healing so you can love your children from a whole place.

Rescued by my Father

My daughter's name is Nala. It means *beloved daughter*. That name is prophetic. It is a declaration over her life. Before she is our beloved daughter, she is God's. And my husband and I want her to always know that. One day, when she was about seven months old, I was driving with her. A Mercedes came spinning out of control. Fast, violent, unpredictable. This was always one of my worst fears: that something would happen, and I wouldn't be able to protect my child. The car was headed straight for us, and I couldn't move. I could only brace for the impact.

But here's the truth: I was wrong that day. I had misjudged the turn. I was following another car and didn't realize that I should not have proceeded. The car was too close. I was in the wrong. It was my mistake. And yet—God. Even when I looked through my rearview mirror, I saw cars swerving off the road, spinning into trees, as they tried to avoid the collision. Chaos was behind me. Impact was in front of me. And still, in my wrong... God intervened. An invisible hand from Heaven stretched down and moved the car that was headed for us. In a moment, the spinning vehicle skipped from in front of us to behind us, and we were untouched.

It was my fault, and God still rescued us. That day wasn't just about a near-death experience; it was a soul-saving moment. I went home, went into the shower, and surrendered my life to Jesus Christ. I have never looked back. In the weakest I had ever felt as a parent, God revealed Himself as the strongest Parent I had ever known. Not just my Father, but my daughter's Father. The One who could do what I never could, what no man could. That day, I didn't just see God; He rescued my soul.

That moment has become a foundational truth in my parenting. I tell my children this: It doesn't matter how wrong you are, or how big the mistake may be, my love for you will not change. I will restore you. Just as God did for me that day and so many other days in my life. He didn't wait for me to be right. He didn't wait for me to fix it. He reached into my mess, into my guilt, into my fear, covered me and extend mercy over and over again. That's the kind of Father I encountered. And that's the kind of love I want my children to experience.

Your children need to know that God is King to the world, God of the Universe, ruler over all, but to us, He is first our Dad. And it is in that place of intimacy and safety that children grow into warriors, because they are first rooted as sons and daughters. The same is true for you and your children. To the world, you may be known by your title or your career. You may be a teacher, a lawyer, an accountant, a therapist, or something else entirely. To the world, you are a servant in that role. But to your children, you are simply Mom. And there is a level of endearment in that name that no title can ever replace.

Just as we cry out to God, "Abba, Father" (Romans 8:15), your children see you not through the lens of what you do for the world, but through the intimacy of who you are to them. That is where safety and identity are formed, in the love and presence of a parent who reflects the heart of the Father.

Children are Arrows — Aim with Intention

"Like arrows in the hand of a warrior are the children of one's youth." (Psalm 127:4, ESV). Your children are the arrows you've been entrusted to launch. They are not meant to sit on display. They are intended to be released. And to be released with purpose, they must be sharpened, aimed, and guided with precision. The goal of parenting isn't control, it's launch. You are not raising children to stay. You are raising arrows to fly and hit their target. This means your assignment as a parent is to disciple them, teach them how to hear God, how to obey, how to forgive, and how to walk uprightly. You are not just raising "good kids". You are raising Kingdom arrows. These arrows are meant to pierce through darkness, establish righteousness, and carry truth wherever they are sent. You must aim with intention.

Arrows don't aim themselves. A child left to themselves will bring shame to their mother (Proverbs 29:15). God gave you those children not just to protect and feed them, but every parent is an archer. The question is: what are you aiming them toward? Don't let the world sharpen your arrows. Don't let culture define their direction. You are the one God trusted to shape them. And you cannot aim well if you're distracted, wounded, bitter, or passive. You must be healed, focused, and aligned with Heaven so you can launch them in the direction of destiny.

Even if you are still growing and healing, that doesn't disqualify you. In fact, your healing can become part of their training. As you learn to obey God in your role as a mother, you're modeling obedience for them. As you learn to submit, forgive, and walk in truth, you are showing them what maturity looks like. They are watching you. More is caught than taught. So, sharpen them well. Pull them back with structure. And when it's time, release them with prophetic accuracy, not into the air, but into assignment.

Raising Spiritual Warriors at Home: Vision, Mission, and Mandate for Your Children

Just as it's essential to have a vision, mission, and mandate for your marriage, it's also important to have one for your children. Raising them isn't just about getting them through school or teaching good manners. It's about stewarding destinies. God has entrusted you with the next generation of Kingdom carriers. And just like a soldier receives orders for an assignment, you, as a parent, should receive Heaven's blueprint for each child. These are questions you should be asking God:

- What is the vision for this child's life?
- What values should we instill?
- What kind of spiritual legacy are they carrying?

Even if you don't yet have a clear prophetic picture of who your children are to God, the Bible gives us a Spirit-breathed blueprint for raising them, just as it does for marriage, friendship, and every other God-ordained relationship.

1. Proverbs 22:6 (ESV)
"Train up a child in the way he should go; even when he is old, he will not depart from it."

This means raising your child according to their unique design and calling. Not forcing them into a mold but guiding them in the way God has wired them to go.

2. Deuteronomy 6:6–7 (NIV)
'These commandments that I give you today are to be on your hearts. Impress them on your children. Talk about them when you

sit at home and when you walk along the road, when you lie down and when you get up."

Parenting is discipleship woven into daily rhythms. God's truth is meant to be impressed on their hearts through lifestyle, not just lectures.

3. Ephesians 6:4 (ESV)
"Fathers, do not provoke your children to anger, but bring them up in the discipline and instruction of the Lord."

Parenting is not about control or behavior management; it's about guiding them in the Lord's ways, with both structure and love.

God's design for parenting is not just about behavior; it's about legacy-building discipleship, raising children who know Him, love Him, and continue His work in the earth. You are not raising children to survive the world; you're raising them to change it. We're not called to just shield them from the fallen world. We're called to equip them to live in it; and to do that, you need to know the enemy. Recognize the cultural lies, distractions, and spiritual warfare that wage war against godly parenting.

Biblical Parents Who Aimed with Purpose

Think about *Mary*, the mother of Jesus. She raised the Savior of the world under Roman occupation, in a culture hostile to the very message He came to bring. Yet Scripture says, "And Jesus increased in wisdom and in stature and in favor with God and man." (Luke 2:52, ESV). That kind of growth doesn't happen without intentional parenting. She guided Him, protected Him, and positioned Him until His appointed time. She didn't focus on protecting Him from pain; she prepared Him for purpose.

Consider the divine preparation in the lives of biblical figures like *Samson and Esther.* In Judges 13, before Samson was even born, the angel of the Lord gave clear instructions to his parents on how to raise him. Their obedience was crucial in preparing Samson to fulfill his calling, even though he didn't always make the right choices. And think of *Esther and Mordecai.* Though not a biological parent and child, Mordecai raised Esther with discernment and wisdom. He counseled her, covered her, and helped her discern her divine moment. Esther wasn't just raised for comfort. She was raised for deliverance. Mordecai helped position her for a moment of national salvation. That's the impact of godly mentorship and parenting.

God often provides guidance, sometimes even before birth, about how to raise children for Kingdom purposes. And He still does this today. Ask Him to reveal the divine assignment for your children and trust Him to guide you as you partner with Heaven in raising them. God has entrusted you with children who have a divine purpose. If you don't raise them in the truth of God's Word, the world will raise them in confusion, potentially derailing the call on their lives.

You are not raising children for comfort or convenience; you're raising them for calling. So, listen for Heaven's guidance, and parent with prophetic precision. The outcome of neglecting their spiritual development is not just behavioral problems; it's generational bondage. But when we intentionally raise them in the fear and knowledge of God, we set them up to be leaders, effective prophets, intercessors, and servants and impactors for Christ. Seek God's strategy. Receive His heart, and remember, you are not just parenting; you are partnering with Heaven to raise sons and daughters who carry the light and power of the Kingdom into the next generation.

When the Arrow Arrives Through Unlikely Circumstances

Not every child enters this world through a story that feels clean, planned, or honored. Some mothers carried their children after deep betrayal, violation, or in a season when they themselves were far from God's blueprint. But God is not limited by how the arrow entered the quiver. Even if your child was conceived through pain or outside the safety of marriage, Heaven assigned purpose to them even before they were placed in your womb. Don't let shame rob you of your authority to aim them well.

The enemy will try to convince you that because of how your child was conceived, you're disqualified from parenting with confidence or calling. But that is a lie. Even if others see your motherhood as accidental, Heaven sees it as intentional. You are still called to raise them with Kingdom vision. God entrusted you, not the situation, to carry that arrow. And if He entrusted you, He equipped you. And because you are the one entrusted, whether your child came into your life through joy or pain, planned or unexpected, your authority as their mother remains. One of the greatest ways to walk in that authority is to pray with them and for them daily.

Pray Together as a Family

Short and simple is fine. Just start the rhythm. It creates safety and spiritual memory. It builds a cadence that your children will return to in times of confusion. Even the shortest prayers, like blessings over dinner, morning covering, or a whispered bedtime "thank you," become roots. These seemingly small moments are how you dig spiritual wells in your home. Over time, the soil becomes saturated with Heaven's presence.

Not too long ago, my son was having difficulties focusing at school, and one day, when I asked him how he did with focus, he said, "I did well because I prayed about it." That moment tickled my heart. He knew he'd been struggling. And at just seven years old, he understood that he was supposed to take that struggle to God. Not only did he pray. He expected an answer. He told me his teacher never had to say anything to him that day. God heard him. Though I gave him a kid-sized crash course on God answering because He is merciful, in that moment, I realized what was happening in our home was what he was carrying into the classroom. This is what it means to train up a child in the way they should go. Prayer doesn't just cover them, it helps them to remember their God is always near, and when they learn that prayer is normal and personal, they begin to see God as real and present in their everyday life.

Let them see you pray when you're tired. Let them hear you ask for wisdom when you're unsure. Let them catch you crying out for help and praising anyway. Don't reserve prayer for moments of crisis. Let it be normal. Because a house that prays together is trained to unlock victory.

Let Your Kids See Reconciliation

Don't just hide the conflict. Let them see how you make peace. Teach them by example how to apologize, forgive, and move forward. Children don't need to see perfect parents; they need to see parents who lean into humility; parents who depend on God's mercy. When your kids watch you hug after an argument, when they hear, "I was wrong. I'm sorry," they begin to understand the gospel at eye level. And even if your husband does not always handle situations like you do, you still have a responsibility as a mother to remember that the children are watching. You remain soft. You remain graceful. You stay grounded in the spirit because your posture is a form of nurturing.

The Bible tells us, "A soft answer turns away wrath, but a harsh word stirs up anger." (Proverbs 15:1, ESV). This is something the Holy Spirit has had to teach me in my own home, especially when everything in me wanted to press further into the argument, and sometimes I do and have to repent. The Holy Spirit would quietly remind me: "The children are listening." And just like that, the Spirit brings me back into alignment with Heaven's way. That gentle whisper has kept me from breaking what I was called to build. Because arguments aren't just moments of frustration, they are moments of formation. If I don't pay attention, one moment of wrath can plant years of fear or instability in my children's hearts. I'm still growing in allowing the Spirit to ground me. Not to perform perfection, but for protection.

Even if your husband is not fully aware of how arguments or raised tones affect the children, I want you to be aware. As the nurturer in your home, you're not just shaping the environment; you're shaping emotional memory. That, too, is part of spiritual warfare. That, too, is ministry. Children often lack the capacity to process things like adults. They easily internalize what they don't understand. While it may be tempting to think, "They're just kids," remember they are sensitive spirit-beings. They are watching, listening, absorbing. And while we don't need to hide everything from them, we must be intentional about what we model.

My husband is actually very good at this. If tension ever arises and the children are nearby, he's the one who will soften the moment. He'll shift the tone, change the atmosphere, or lighten the mood because he understands that what our children witness can become a part of them. They have such tender hearts that if they hear us speaking in a higher tone, they might immediately say, "Stop fighting!" even when we're not arguing. And we have to reassure them: "We're not fighting, we're just having a conversation." It's in those moments that we're reminded that what seems small to us can feel big to them. So be mindful. Guard the atmosphere. You don't have to be loud to be heard. You don't have to dominate to lead. As a woman, as a wife, as a mother, be soft. Be gracious. Be feminine. It looks good on you.

Make the Atmosphere Reflect Heaven

Music, peace, laughter, prayer, worship, boundaries. Your home should feel like a place where God lives. Let it be a sanctuary of joy and rest. Heaven's presence is not just ethereal, it's tangible. Let worship music set the tone. Let softness be the fragrance. Let laughter echo through the walls like a song of praise. Let boundaries create peace, not pressure. Even if you're not playing worship music, play clean music. Sounds that carry life, not confusion. Let the lyrics that fill your home speak truth, joy, and love. Avoid playing music that's demeaning or contains messages that contradict the Spirit of God. Remember, atmosphere is prophetic. It sets the tone for what your children will absorb and replay in their hearts.

You can still enjoy variety. For example, in our home, we have a fondness for reggae music. Sometimes, you'll hear uplifting reggae, not because it's labeled "Christian," but because it's clean, uplifting, and joyful, and remind us of our homeland, Jamaica. The beat carries rhythm, but the words carry peace. That's the key. Whether it's gospel, jazz, acoustic, or instrumental, let it uplift. Let it edify. Let it feel like Heaven would sit there. Because the environment you cultivate shapes the expectations your children will carry about what life with God is supposed to feel like. You are their first sanctuary; build with beauty and intention.

Becoming a Safe Place of Confession and Conversation

Just as we can come to God as our Father to confess our sins, to be restored, and to experience mercy, we must also become that place for our children. Yes, there may be consequences for what they've done wrong, but even in correction, God's heart is always restoration. That is the model we are called to carry into our homes. We should not be so quick to punish that we forget to restore. We should not be so eager to discipline that we miss the opportunity to disciple. The goal is not just behavior change; it's heart transformation. Like we talked about before, we want our children to know that when they fall short, they can come to us with truth and find mercy, not condemnation; that we are a place they can run to, not hide from.

If we don't create that safe place of confession in our homes, they'll find it elsewhere. And the danger is not just what they'll do; it's who they'll trust when they don't believe they can trust us. We want to be the first place they run when they don't know what to do. That means listening more than lecturing, creating space for honesty, and being quick to redeem, not just quick to correct.

When Tender Hearts Confess

My oldest child is only ten years old, so I may not be able to relate to the older years of parenting through experience, but there are stages in parenting that feel both beautiful and terrifying. For me, it is now, when my daughter hit the double digits—that sensitive age where they are no longer little but not yet fully grown. Their hearts are tender, their emotions are stretching, and school, friends, and the world begin to expose them to things you wish you could protect them from.

I remember when my daughter came to me and began sharing things that I was not ready to hear. In that moment, I wanted to be a safe place for her confession, but inside I was praying, "Lord Jesus, help me. Give me the strength to listen without fear or shock, without shutting her down. Give me the right words to say. Help me affirm her, and let my words be stronger than the lies she believes."

As parents, we do not always feel ready for what our children carry in their hearts. But this is where our complete dependence on Jesus comes in. I cannot be her safe place apart from Him. My wisdom is not enough. My composure is not enough. My love alone is not enough. But when I lean on Christ, His grace holds me steady. His mercy teaches me how to listen. His Spirit gives me the words to say or the silence to hold.

Parenting is not about having it all together. It is about pointing our children to the One who holds it all together, our Lord Jesus. His grace bounces us back up when we falter, and His mercy never lets us go. When we depend on Him, we can be the safe space our children need, even when we feel unprepared. That is the kind of parent we should long to be—not perfect, but anchored in the One who is.

Confidentiality matters too. When your child entrusts you with something and asks you not to share it, honoring that request helps protect the bond of trust. I have learned this in part because of my relationship with God as Father. I treasure sonship so deeply, and I know the safety of being able to confess to Him my darkest moments, my mistakes, and my mess. God never recoils, and He never exposes me. He covers me, counsels me, and loves me in the midst of it. That intimacy with Him has shaped how I parent. It has taught me that the same Father who is a safe place for me equips me to be a safe place for my children. What they need, He has already placed in me, or it's within reach. The same mercy and presence I experience with God, I now get to extend to them.

Pay attention to how God is speaks to you about your children. Many times, the Lord has given me dreams and insights, warnings, confirmations, and all I had to do was start a conversation. I didn't need to accuse or probe; I simply opened the door, and they walked through it with honesty. Be sensitive. Make time for intentional conversations. Sit at the table and ask questions. Look them in the eyes. Notice shifts in mood. Don't assume silence means everything is okay. Dig deeper. Invite honesty with gentleness.

My husband and I often describe ourselves as farmers in our children's lives. We can't control every seed thrown at them out in the world, at school, church, in the community, among friends. But when they come home, we get to till the soil, pull the weeds, and indirectly ask, "What was planted today that doesn't belong?" and then uproot, and replant truth in its place.

One day my daughter suddenly refused to wear the fitted gym pants I had just bought and instead wanted only bell-bottom styles, or baggy pants. Frustrated, I asked why she'd let me spend money on clothes she wouldn't wear. Finally, she admitted the reason: a boy at school told her she had "thick thighs." That was the weed!

My mama-bear reaction came out before my holy one did—I blurted, "that's a stupid thing to say, is he a stupid boy?" My daughter burst into laughter. I quickly repented for my choice of words, but in that moment, the laughter broke the weight off her. Then I said, "Next time someone says something that makes you feel bad about yourself, stop and ask: Who is the source? Do they even know what they're talking about? Is this coming from someone wise and trustworthy?" She shook her head no. "Exactly! He's about ten-year-old, what could he possibly know about thighs? Your thighs are beautiful, and just right for you."

That's what spiritual parenting looks like. It's not just rules and routines; it's relationship. It's daily gardening, Spirit-led conversations that prune, protect, and water the heart of your child with life-giving truth. So be the safe place. Be the parent who reflects the mercy and wisdom of God. Let your home be a sanctuary where truth is told, correction is gentle, and the voice of the Lord is never crowded out. Normalize apologizing to your children. As parents, sometimes we mess up too. Forgive yourself and don't dwell on what your children haven't grasped yet. Thank God for what He's doing and do your best. Trust the Holy Spirit to lead you step by step.

Boundaries Are Protection, Not Punishment

In my opinion, lack of rules and lack of discipline is child abuse. Every home should have discipline, a disciplinary method for your children, and rules that govern them. Rules are not to restrict their joy; they are to protect their life and destiny. Just like God gives us commandments in the Bible for our own good, we are called to do the same for our children. The truth is: there's always a war going on between light and darkness, and rules provide the boundaries that help keep our children within the safety of wisdom, away from spiritual danger. You may say, "Why do I need to give them a curfew?" Because the streets have no mercy when the sun goes down. You're not trying to raise perfect children, but you are trying to protect them and prepare them for life.

Our children will make mistakes. They will fail sometimes, and that's expected. Because failure teaches, and mistakes produce maturity. More importantly, they create space for them to appreciate grace and mercy. As parents, our prayer should not just be for perfection, but for perspective. We must say, "Lord, when they fall, help them to learn. Help them rise again. Don't let them remain where they fall; bring them back to You, just like the prodigal son. Let them remember who they are, and whose they are. Let our home always be a place where they know they can return to love, grace, and restoration."

As you enforce boundaries, teach your children that they don't need to hide from you. Show them what it looks like to be corrected without being crushed. Let them see that the rules are not walls; they are safety nets. Let them know that your discipline doesn't come from rejection, but from revelation. Because the way you receive their honesty, their struggles, and their growing process may shape the way they believe God receives theirs. You are not raising rule-followers. You are raising truth-lovers; children who know the boundaries and the love that holds them up.

Parenting in Partnership: Honor, Order, and Grace

The Bible makes it clear that agreement matters: "Can two walk together, unless they are agreed?" (Amos 3:3, NKJV). That truth also applies to parenting. Ideally, husband and wife should raise their children in agreement, bringing different perspectives into alignment through shared prayer, revelation, and open communication. If you and your husband were raised differently, it is important to decide together how you will parent intentionally, shaping your home from revelation rather than just reacting out of tradition or pain.

But let's be honest. Not every marriage has that rhythm. Not every home has a united parenting strategy or a shared understanding of spiritual order. For some, parenting looks like navigating shared custody. Not every child lives in a two-parent household, and some children move between two homes because of separation or divorce. Some women are walking this journey without much guidance from their spouse.

This book is written for all of you. Even if your husband does not yet carry the same spiritual conviction or revelation. Even if you and your child's father are not co-parenting well. You can still fulfill your assignment with grace. Remain submitted to God, do what is required of you, and allow Him to do the rest. You can still walk in wisdom and see fruit in your children's lives because of your obedience. Humble yourself, pursue peace, and trust God to cover the gaps.

There are moments when my husband handles a parenting situation differently than I would have. And everything in me wants to say, "Why did you do it that way?" But I've learned to bite my tongue, hold my peace, and speak privately later, after the children are asleep and emotions have calmed. Disagreement doesn't have to become disorder. Unity doesn't mean sameness; it means alignment.

In fact, something like this just happened in our home this week. My son was getting ready for school, and we were running behind. He had already stepped into the shower, no clothes on, shower running, and his dad was using bathroom at the same time. When my son said he needed to pee, my husband, trying to move things along, said, "Just let him pee in the shower." From his perspective, it was quick and harmless. He was in the bath and the water was already running. But I didn't feel right about it. We went back and forth for a moment, and I gently said, "Can you just trust me? Let him step out of the shower, and I'll explain later."

Later that day, I sent my husband a text, not to correct him, but to share my heart. I reminded him, "We're not just raising him to live comfortably in our home, we're raising him to function respectfully in the world." I explained that we want to train him now to be mindful of shared spaces. One day he may be in someone else's home, and what feels normal to us might feel disrespectful or unhygienic to others. I even shared that when I was in college, things like this were strongly emphasized. We were repeatedly told not to treat shared spaces casually, especially bathrooms and dorm areas. That memory stuck with me. I just didn't want to plant a habit now that could create embarrassment or conflict later. My husband texted back, "Thank you, baby. That makes so much sense." Our roles are not in competition with each other. They're in completion. We're on the same team, even if we see from different angles.

As women, we are called to walk in both wisdom and submission. It's not silence. It's a spiritual strategy. It's knowing when to speak, and what spirit you're speaking from. There's nothing dishonorable about bringing your concerns to your husband. But timing and tone matter. Especially when little eyes are watching. Even when you disagree with how something was handled, let your children see respect. Let them see you honor their father, even if you process differently behind the scenes. Because what they see becomes what they replicate. And if you undermine their father's voice in front of them, you unknowingly undermine your own authority as well.

It's not always easy. Sometimes what you're holding back feels like fire in your bones. But submission doesn't mean you're weak, it means you're surrendered. Surrendered to God's order. Surrendered to preserving peace. Surrendered to handling disagreements in the Spirit and not the flesh. At the same time, your voice matters. You are not invisible. God gave your children two parents for a reason. And you were given to your husband as a helper—ezer, in the Hebrew, a word that describes a divine ally, a strong support, a necessary presence. When you bring insight to the table, bring it boldly, but bring it wisely. Not in front of the children. Not with sarcasm or contempt. But with love, timing, and truth.

If the two of you are constantly clashing about parenting, set a rhythm for private check-ins. Maybe after the children go to bed, take 15 minutes to regroup. Ask each other, "How do you think we handled that?" Talk it out. Pray it out. Even cry it out if needed. But come back to alignment. Because unity between parents creates emotional stability in children.

We are parenting on the same team, not just as spouses, but as co-laborers in the Kingdom. Our goal is not just to raise obedient children, but whole ones. And that requires partnership, pursuit, and agreement. So, choose honor, humility, and unity, not just for your marriage, but for your children's future.

Prayer

Father, heal the places in me that were not loved well as a child. Where rejection, neglect, or pain shaped my heart, bring Your love and restoration. Don't let the brokenness of my past become the pattern of my parenting. Teach me how to give to my children what I may not have fully received and fill every gap with Your presence. Show me how to sharpen my children, guide them, and release them at the appointed time. Give me discernment, patience, and grace as I parent with purpose. Help me honor my role in the home even when I feel unseen or misunderstood. May my heart remain soft, and my spirit stay aligned with Yours. Let my home be a training ground for warriors of the Kingdom. And let the fruit of obedience show up in my children for generations. In Jesus' name, Amen.

Journal Reflection

In what ways has your own childhood trained you for how to love your children, and in what ways has it made love harder to give?

In what area is God asking you to sharpen your children right now?

What habits, attitudes, or patterns in your home are helping or hindering their aim?

How can you intentionally aim your children toward their God-ordained purpose?

Is there a parenting disagreement you've been navigating that needs to be brought to God first?

What can you do this week to honor unity, even if complete agreement has not yet been reached?

Take a moment to reflect on the parenting dynamic in your home. Are there areas where you and your husband are not in agreement?

Rather than trying to change him, ask the Holy Spirit to show you where you can walk in wisdom, timing, and grace.

Tactical Tip:
Journal one area where your child needs sharpening; whether in discipline, faith, or responsibility.

Pray and ask the Lord how you can lovingly support that development this week.

CONCLUSION

STANDING GUARD

After the Battle, the Guard Remains

In the military, the end of a battle does not mean the end of vigilance. Soldiers return to base, but their weapons stay close, patrols continue, and the guard posts remain manned. Why? Because the enemy doesn't need a full assault to cause damage, he only needs an open gate. True soldiers learn to live ready: not fearful, but focused. Not frantic, but watchful. Marriage is no different. Just because tension has eased, or peace has returned doesn't mean your assignment as a guard is over. You are still on duty. As a wife, you are not simply someone who survived battles; you are someone God has entrusted to protect what He restored. This is not about living in survival mode. This is about remaining in position.

You're Already Equipped, Stay Alert

This is not a call to pressure; it is a reminder of who you already are. If you've made it this far through the pages of this book, it's because God has already begun a deep work in you. You are a wife with spiritual insight. You don't need another title, platform, or layer of confirmation. You already have the grace to guard what God has given you.

Spiritual warfare does not mean living in a constant state of battle. It means living with awareness. The enemy rarely attacks loudly; more often, he waits for distraction, disconnection, or spiritual laziness to slip in unnoticed. God calls you to be alert, not afraid. Remain prayerful, discerning, and Spirit-led.

What Standing Guard Looks Like

Standing guard as a wife is not always dramatic warfare. Often, it looks like faithful stewardship:

- Start with a spiritual check-in. Ask the Holy Spirit what's happening in your home.

- Pay attention to patterns. Repeated tensions are warnings, not coincidences.

- Stay in the Word. Scripture keeps your spirit sharp and your authority strong.

- Pray before reacting. Refuse to let the enemy bait you into fighting flesh.

- Protect unity. If something feels "off," seek God's perspective before assuming the worst.

You are not just a wife; you are a gatekeeper, that notice things, and deal with them in prayer, with wisdom, and with authority. As a watchman, you will see what others don't and you will sound the alarm when danger approaches. You are discerning and ready.

Prayer

Father, thank You for trusting me with this home, this marriage, and this role. Keep me from distraction and discouragement. Remind me that I already have Your grace to guard what You've given me. I will not live in fear, but I will stay awake. Strengthen me to remain in position, in Jesus' name, Amen.

Journal Reflection
Ask yourself:

- Am I staying alert, or just staying busy?
- Have I ignored anything God has been showing me?
- Where is God asking me to watch with fresh eyes?

A Final Commission

As you close this book, remember this: God has already sent you. You are already appointed. Already positioned on the wall of your marriage and your family. You don't need permission or recognition to pray and intercede. You don't need a platform to walk in power. God entrusted you with that husband, those children, and that atmosphere. Stand, not because things are perfect, but because you are assigned.

Your marriage is more than a relationship. It is an assignment. It carries a vision, fulfills a mission, and answers a mandate from Heaven. Every prayer you've prayed, every sacrifice you've made, every shift you've embraced; it has never been just about today. It has always been about the eternal assignment. So, stand, because you were sent. Guard, because you were chosen. Love, because you were first loved. And as you do, may your home be a base of Kingdom power for generations to come

ABOUT THE AUTHOR

Tamminn S. Trail is a wife, mother, social worker (MSW), and minister of the gospel whose heart burns to see women flourish in God's design for identity, marriage, and motherhood. Originally from Ocho Rios, Jamaica, she now lives with her husband of twelve years, Tyrone, and their children, Nala and Micah, on Long Island, New York. Out of her own journey of surrender through seasons of grief, obedience, and revelation, she equips women to live in the fullness of God's intent for their lives and to build families that carry His legacy.

The breaking point of her journey came with the loss of her daughter, Zoe, whose very name means life. Though Zoe never took a breath on earth, her presence stirred an eternal purpose: a call to multiply the life that only Christ gives. That life continues to flow through Tamminn as a wife, a mother, and a daughter of God, and it now multiplies as she pours out all God has placed within her so that women and families everywhere may flourish in His design.

Her work is published through T.S. Trail, a faith-based publishing company dedicated to helping women flourish in God's design for identity, marriage, and motherhood. Through its books, courses, and prophetic teaching, T.S. Trail exists to extend that mission and build Kingdom legacy for families everywhere.

You can discover more about her at: www.tstrail.com. You can also connect with her personally on social media at @TamminnTrail (Instagram, Facebook, TikTok).